First published in 2017 by

Schism prɛss²

First edition
ISBN: 978-1543166231

Cover design by GJS
Frontispiece: 'The Beheading of St. John The Baptist' (detail) by
Giovanni di Paolo

Printed in London, UK.

For Elias & Nadja Merhige

We are the limbs of that head. This body cannot be decapitated.

– St. Augustine.

SACER

Nicola Masciandaro

FADE IN:

EXT. A SMALL ISLAND ON THE SEINE (March 18, 1314)
– EVENING

The bodies of two men burn at the stake. Tied to separate poles, the torsos have slumped over so that their heads nearly touch. In the distance is the skyline of medieval Paris.

A crowd stands and lingers in silence. Multicolored flames lick the blackened, charred remains.[1] Smoke and ashes mingle in the evening air before a golden sunset. The mystery of dead life floating between matter and light. A Franciscan FRIAR stands before the pyre holding a metal Tau crucifix upon a pole at eye-level to the bodies. The flared form of the cross is similar to the cross patteé of the Templars.[2] We zoom in slowly, centered on a point between the corpses' skulls.

> BYSTANDER
> See the heretic love-birds! Even in death they want to kiss!

There is laughter and jeering from the crowd, shouts of "idolaters," "sodomites" and "blasphemers." Two SOLDIERS step forward on either side of the FRIAR with long poles to stoke the fire.

LEFT SOLDIER
Templar flesh is tougher than a peacock's![3]

RIGHT SOLDIER
Maybe the friar's cross saves it from the flame.

LEFT SOLDIER
The deeper to burn in hell!

The burning progresses and the skeletons blacken and smoke as the flames die down. The camera zooms in slowly. A DARK FIGURE emerges from the shadows and removes a thigh bone from one of the skeletons.[4] Black ash swirls in the burning air. Closer and closer we zoom in slower and slower motion, until we see a single moving mote of black ash, so that it appears as if our vision collides with it in mid-air. We then pass immediately *into* the interior of a black pyramid, so as to produce the sense of a dimensional inversion of space and time.[5] Inside, the four triangular walls of the pyramid are deep black, like onyx, while the floor appears immaterial, a groundless ground of luminous void criss-crossed with veins of oblivion or dark matter. All the angles of the pyramid, as well as the diagonals on the square base glow with a golden light. At the center of the X created by the diagonals on the floor, a small glass-like ocular sphere projects patterns of tiny dots on the four walls of the pyramid. We pass through the pyramid and are now moving in the opposite direction, zooming away from as if having passed through a mirror, without turning around. We are now inside of a small, square white stone temple, the camera hovering as if it is itself a mote of dust suspended in the air. In the center of the temple is a stone basin into which a fine black dust is gathering into a small pile, drawn by a mysterious magnetism. The camera zooms into the dust on a similar path then goes black.

EXT. HILLSIDE WITH SMALL, SHALLOW CAVE NEAR ASSISI (SEPTEMBER 29, 1978) – PREDAWN

THREE FIGURES assemble via automobiles at the end of a road in the autumnal Umbrian countryside. They wear distinct black clothing, in a style somewhere between neo-medieval and fascist, but without shoes or gloves. They walk up to the cave, which shows no signs of human presence. After a few quiet words, one of them enters the cave, takes from a small reliquary a cylindrical piece of charcoal and draws on the wall a cross-like geometric image suggestive of both the human form and a face. They gather around the drawing, stare at it for a short while, then enter the drawing one by one, vanishing through the wall.

INT. PAPAL APARTMENTS, POPE'S PRIVATE STUDY – SUNRISE

One by one the THREE FIGURES enter the study through a Renaissance painting of Christ on a Tau cross (Andrea Solario's *Crucifixion* would work)[6] whose proportions match the drawing in the cave. The POPE, seated over a cappuccino and an old book (*The Spiritual Exercise of St. Ignatius of Loyola*) is briefly surprised but then calm, as if he intuitively knows what is happening. The POPE tears a piece of parchment from the inside over of the book. We see, briefly, that the parchment contains a pattern of small circles containing Arabic numbers in radiating lines.

ONE OF THE THREE FIGURES
Servus servorum!

POPE
Into your hands I commend my spirit.
    (handing the parchment to one of the THREE FIGURES)

Two of the THREE FIGURES remove from the wall a life-sized crucifix, dismember the statue of Christ upon it, then set the cross on the ground. The POPE gets up and lays himself upon it. They begin to drive nails into his hands and feet, one FIGURE at his feet, and one at each of his hands.

THREE FIGURES
With this crime, we absolve you. With your sin, our hands are clean. There is no sin . . .

POPE
Forgive them, for they *know* what they are doing.

After the POPE is elevated upside down on the cross,[7] the FIGURE at the POPE's left hand takes out a small pouch of ashes and pours it into the POPE's mouth, nostrils, eyes, and ears. The FIGURE at the right hand readies a short sword to decapitate the POPE.

THREE FIGURES
(in unison)
Super non contra.[8] There is no we![9]

The POPE's head falls to the ground bathed in his own spurting blood, which mixes with the ashes as his mouth audibly says, "Elijah, Elijah."[10] The THREE FIGURES shout, "Arna Dei." Once the head is severed, the FIGURE who was at the POPE's feet cuts into his side near his heart and places the piece of parchment deep inside. We zoom into the POPE's eyes, through his pupils, then into the fire-lit face of St. Peter as he denies Christ before the cock crows,[11] then through Peter's eyes into a vision of Jesus on the cross in a cosmic void, saying, "Why have you forsaken me?" The camera zooms into Christ's body, revealing a dark abstract corridor of lenses reminiscent of the interior of both a camera and a tomb, followed by a flash of light.

INT. FRANK MASTRO'S APARTMENT, LOWER EAST SIDE, MANHATTAN, BEDROOM (SEPTEMBER 7, PRESENT DAY) – EARLY MORNING

FRANK wakes as if startled by the vision of the previous scene. He stares into space for a moment, then turns on the light, reaches for a notebook, and starts writing.

INT. OCULUS MEDIA LABORATORIES, CALIFORNIA – MORNING

RICHARD OVERBY is leading an international group of investors on a tour through the Oculus Media laboratories. He brings them to a circular room at the center of which is an MRI machine, which is colored and lit to accentuate its resemblance to the human eye. On either side of the MRI are two MEG machines, all black in color, with their characteristic drop-down screens. The investors gather in a semi-circle, RICHARD stands in the center.

                    RICHARD
For as long as humans have existed, we have sought to make dreams a reality. That is what makes our species so special. But there is one dream that still eludes us, a dream which escapes us because it is already real, a horizon we cannot reach because it is too close. I speak of the dream of dreaming itself, of being able to dream, with the full power of imagination, while we are awake.

The investors stir in approving anticipation.

                 RICHARD (cont'd)
Now, thanks to recent breakthroughs in research conducted in this laboratory, Oculus Media stands at the threshold of making this dream come true.

Two identical TWINS enter the room from behind the MRI and stand next to the MEG machines. They are wearing simple dresses, Egyptian necklaces with symmetrical Eye of Horus designs, and are holding mask-like objects.

> RICHARD (cont'd)
> Please welcome Emma and Gemma, who will demonstrate our discovery. The time is soon when we will not only watch cinema, but *dream* it, envisioning our vision in real time with the full power of the imagination operating in a state we call AS, 'acute subjectivity.'[12] Never again will special effects not be good enough—they will be better. Never again will a film not exceed your expectations. The sky is no longer the limit when we don't look up there, but in *here*.
> (pointing to his head)
> Ladies.

The TWINS place the masks on their heads, covering their eyes and ears.

> RICHARD (cont'd)
> These are prototypes of the Oculus mask, used to deliver the *matrix of impressions* necessary to sync with the embedded cinema protocols. Delivered audio-visually, these impressions are harmless and non-interactive. Unlike our would-be competitors, Oculus is committed to 100% non-invasive, pure neurocinema. Let's keep the brain implants where they belong, in the movies.

INT. FRANK MASTRO'S APARTMENT, LOWER EAST SIDE, MANHATTAN – MIDDAY

FRANK goes to his study, opens a book at his desk, and plays an old Italian song, "Melancolie in Settembre" by Peppino di Capri.[13] After a moment, he leans over as if peering into something. We see a tear fall onto a small mirror. FRANK picks up his phone and takes a picture of the tear. He turns off the song, brings up the picture on his computer screen, and zooms in as if looking for something. The heart-like form of a face is visible.[14] He gets a beautifully framed photograph of his dead daughter ASTRA, which was shot on the Brooklyn Bridge, and holds it next to the photograph. There is a similarity, but there is also something subtly demonic about the face. FRANK prints out the image and then draws over it with a pencil the outline of the eyes, the double lines of the front of the nose, and the nose-to-mouth lines, so that the design resembles a winged creature and also a cross, like a seraph, close to the form used by the THREE FIGURES in the opening scene. As FRANK gazes into the design, the camera hovers behind and above his head, and then around the room in an unusual way, not directing us to anything in particular, but suggesting the spontaneous drift of consciousness outside the body as one's imagination is activated. The small study is rather messy, crammed with books and papers and various objects. A number of storyboard drawings are visible and other film-related objects, including an Italian poster for *Forsaken* ("Desolato" in Italian), the lettering of which gives prominence to the letters S-O-L. He kisses the photograph of ASTRA.

INT. OCULUS MEDIA LABORATORIES, CALIFORNIA – MORNING (cont'd)

There are approving chuckles from the INVESTORS, one of whom raises his hand.

MR. KAGO
Mr. Overby?

RICHARD
Yes, Mr. Kago. Please, call me Richard.

MR. KAGO

Is the matrix always the same, or are different configurations possible?

RICHARD

We are working to maximize customizability, so that users will be able to select and even design their own impression patterns, similar to a stereo equalizer.

MRS. RINEHART

Are there any side-effects?

RICHARD

No. The impressions are entirely used up or spent in the process of projective viewing. And they are active only in the presence of Oculus's unique sequencing algorithm, so no worries about seeing ghosts when you pause the film to get a snack.

Chuckles from the crowd.

MS. JOSHI

How does this affect film production?

RICHARD

Almost everything is done in the editing lab. But we also work directly with actors, who must be specially trained to deliver psychic cues which are synchronized to the impressional matrix. This is what generates the affective depth of our neurocinematic experience, setting it apart from mere visual effects. Later you will have a chance to meet Robert Mastro, the star of Max Sleiman's latest film, *Kingdom of Night* – and my stepson – who is working with Oculus in this capacity.

Signs of excitement. A small green light illuminates on each of the TWIN's masks

RICHARD (cont'd)
OK. Gemma, Emma.

The TWINS sit in their respective MEG machines, increasing their resemblance to Egyptian goddesses. The screens in front of them start to show a film, casting light on their faces. Other screens in the room show the scans of their brain functions.

RICHARD (cont'd)
As you can see, they are now observing the same film. Let's turn our attention to the dorsolateral prefrontal cortex.

RICHARD presses a button on a remote control to zoom in on the MEG read out screens.

RICHARD (cont'd)
This is the region of the brain responsible for the lucid dreaming state. Both cortexes are highly active, but there are marked differences in patterning. If Gemma's imagination is a panther, Emma's is a gazelle. This degree of variance is otherwise unachievable, not without the application of psycho-active substances. In other words, we are now seeing, beyond a shadow of a doubt, that the minds of our Oculus-imprinted viewers are watching *essentially different films*.

The INVESTORS quietly applaud.

ANONYMOUS INVESTOR
Impressive. But they are not conscious of this, is that correct?

                    RICHARD
Only partially, Mr. X. We have yet to actualize the neurocinema interface to full awareness levels. However,
unaccountable presences and lucid sensory memories,
positive signs of immanent projective viewing, are recorded. But at present, only twenty-one percent of our
subjects report . . . seeing things. With the help of our
new research partners in Rome, we hope to turn the
corner toward total seamless AS by next spring. On that
note, let us proceed to the reception where the ladies
may share with you their impressions of the Oculus experience.

RICHARD leads the TWINS and the group of INVESTORS
out. We see them pass before the camera as if we are staying
behind. Once all have left, the camera makes a full pan of the
circular room in silence.

EXT. COFFEE SHOP IN BROOKLYN – MIDDAY

GARY THATCHER and ARIANA FOX at a cafe. They sit
silhouetted against the window, facing each other with their
laptops out, in such a way that the street scene outside feels
screenic and cinematically framed.

                    ARIANA
You had that dream again last night, didn't you?

                    GARY
How did you know?

                    ARIANA
Something in your gaze, like it's been . . . crushed.

GARY looks at ARIANA in an intense way.

ARIANA

Are you still going to Brooklyn College to speak with that film studies professor?

GARY

Yes, Frank Mastro, the director of *Forsaken*.

ARIANA

The one with the crazy beheading scene?

GARY

More like "miraculous." Effects that real do not happen by accident. I don't think he knows what he did.

ARIANA

I still don't get it. You are saying that he actually filmed his imagination?

GARY

In a way. More like the camera saw a vision carried upon the light, like a television wave.

ARIANA

OK.

GARY

Why don't you come with me today? It will be fun and he'll see what I mean more clearly with you there. "And she will be a light between truth and your intellect."[15]

ARIANA

Hmm?

GARY

Something Virgil says about Beatrice to Dante in Purgatory. Nevermind, a way of saying . . .

21

ARIANA

Sweet. But no I think this is more you than me.

GARY

Our eyes receive, reflect, and project. Haven't you ever talked to someone just by gazing?

ARIANA

Maybe in a dream.

GARY winks. We see the reflection of his computer screen in his eyes.

ARIANA

See the reflection of all in all.

GARY

Nice one. That's how it really is. The world is cinema, universal studios.[16]

ARIANA

Picture everything with the camera of me. Like Plato's cave?[17]

GARY

Exactly. I am the video of my own beheading.[18]

ARIANA

Weird. You lost me, or I lost myself.

GARY

Not weirder than being here in the first place.

ARIANA

That's why I love you, because you found I in the first place. So what about *Forsaken*?

BARISTA
(overhearing)
Are you guys are talking about *Forsaken*? I gotta show you my tattoo.

The BARISTA walks over and shows his tattoo: a naked woman holding her own severed head with three streams of blood flowing out into her own head's mouth and the mouths of two other figures, male and female.

ARIANA
No way. Behead me in four dimensions.[19]

BARISTA
What?

ARIANA
Nothing, just writing to myself. Hey, you and I, twin tattoos? Cheaper than a ring.

GARY
Uh, think I will be going now.

ARIANA
OK, see you tonight. I love you!

GARY
Eye love you [silently mouthing 'love you'].

INT. PSYCHOTHERAPIST'S OFFICE, MALIBU – LATE MORNING

SAMANTHA OVERBY is seated comfortably before DR. GOLDSMITH, who is wearing a turtleneck under his blazer and has an egg-shaped sculpture on his desk.

DR. GOLDSMITH
Happy birthday, Samantha.

SAMANTHA
Thank you.

DR. GOLDSMITH
How have you been since our last session?

SAMANTHA
OK. September is not easy for me. And I always seem to remember my birthday in the wrong way.

DR. GOLDSMITH
What do you mean?

SAMANTHA
Like everything never stops happening in September, including me.

DR. GOLSMITH
Sometimes the impossible totality of things catches up with us. Is there anything in particular? You said "it."

SAMANTHA
I don't know. I left New York in September, and Robert's father. But that was years ago.

DR. GOLDSMITH
Do you miss New York?

SAMANTHA
Not really, not Frank. He is coming out next week to visit for the first time, for the premiere.

DR. GOLDSMITH
But you two communicate don't you?

SAMANTHA
Not really. Not since I left. But he knows it was for the best.

DR. GOLDSMITH
That only makes it harder. The wounded pride of a father.

SAMANTHA
And the pride of a wounded father. That was the root of it, the drinking, drowning in sorrow over his firstborn.

DR. GOLDSMITH
And how is Robert? He must be excited.

SAMANTHA
Totally. He has worked so hard for this. And Richard too. He is so happy for him, like he was his own.

DR. GOLDSMITH
Well that covers the men. What about you? How is your art going?

SAMANTHA
Frustrating. But I realized something recently. A friend told me the sculpture I was working on looked like a dead fetus.

DR. GOLDSMITH
Yes?

SAMANTHA
Well, because my concept was totally different but she

only saw something . . . lifeless. Anyway, so we talk more about it and she breaks down, sobbing. It turns out that she had an abortion a long time ago and never talked about it.

DR. GOLDSMITH
So she projected the suppressed experience onto your sculpture. That is normal.

SAMANTHA
Yes, but the strange thing is, she was totally right. I couldn't see it. Then she said something that stuck with me, that what haunts her is not the killing of life, but taking away its chance to cry. The silence of it.

DR. GOLDSMITH
Interesting. Is this how you feel?

SAMANTHA
Like there's this enormous sea inside which I use art to *not* express, to keep at bay. It's all twisted. Does that make sense?

DR. GOLDSMITH
Our true self gets buried under an identity, a concept, which blocks spontaneity, creativity. One must stay in touch with that inner abyss, the trauma of being born.[20] Otherwise . . .

SAMANTHA
So I've started a whole new body of work, a series of emergent life forms in the shape of tears.

DR. GOLDSMITH
Wonderful. Today really is your birthday. We are born every day. And this sounds like a beautiful way to cele-

brate it.

SAMANTHA

Well it is too early to celebrate, but OK. I am still worried.

DR. GOLDSMITH

Exactly, *you* are worried.[21] So let's talk more about your fears. That is why we are here.

SAMANTHA

But should I be? I mean, am *I* why I am here? I really don't know.

DR. GOLDSMITH

Who does?

SERIES OF SHOTS – FRANK EN ROUTE TO THE COLLEGE – MIDDAY

Along the way we see things related to the intersection of head, vision, and camera: the MTA's "If you see something, say something" security notice; commuters absorbed in their hand-held devices; a film poster for Drone, a Hollywood film with tag-line "you'll never see it coming"; security cameras mounted on poles; a Go-Pro style headcam display in a shop window; and finally, a newspaper cover with a still from the latest terrorist beheading video. The shots should give a sense of the quotidian horror of life.

EXT/INT. MOUNTAIN LODGE, NEW HAMPSHIRE – MIDDAY

MARSILIO BARBI, in a green suit, stands in his office surveying the landscape, then returns to his desk where he has been examining an array of mathematical formulas, geometric diagrams, and data sheets. Placed prominently among them is a facsimile of the blood-stained parchment placed inside the Pope's body, as well as a schematic diagram based on it that resembles the Prime Number Cross, shaded to accentuate its resemblance to the Templar cross.[22] There is also a map of Rome, with a transparent overlay of a complex of ley lines radiating and intersecting through the Vatican. The overlay is dated "28 Settembre 1978." At the other side of the room, CLAUDIA BRANDINI sits on an old, somewhat Masonic-styled chair. She wears black, gold jewelry, and is petting a white cat while studying an old book on a stand placed next to the chair. MARSILIO picks up the phone.

RICHARD

Marsilio.

MARSILIO

Richard, hi. I will not make Max's premiere this weekend. Much to do here. Claudia is still coming of course, for two days.

[CLAUDIA smiles and shifts in her chair]

She will carry the Sybil's key. You are given access for one hour on Sunday the 13th, Robert for 7 minutes. Follow Claudia's instructions to the letter. She will record.

RICHARD

I will.

MARSILIO

Enjoy! And no lies. The channel must be kept clean.

RICHARD

I understand. As before.

MARSILIO

She will use a new name. See that she has everything

she needs. And intimate nothing, especially to Frank.

RICHARD

OK. But I doubt Mastro retains anything of the 1978 transmission. Our analyses shows that the *Forsaken* effects were epiphenomenal, only an echo.

MARSILIO

Data cannot grasp the depth of such images, which do not pass away or cease bleeding into things.

RICHARD

Robert is ours and Samantha confirms that whatever inspiration Frank conducted died with the child. I do not see the danger.

MARSILIO

How can you? The girl's death gave time to grow Oculus. But that was 1987, and she or he will soon be within three years of thirty-three in the next body, likely to re-establish contact and minister latent DGI impressions from the '78 discharge.

RICHARD

DGI?

MARSILIO

Dispensatio gratiae imaginalis.

RICHARD

So eliminate Frank.

MARSILIO

Richard! Please, it is not so simple as your American spirit wants. That would be riskier than you can imagine. Then we lose the thread, the potential of weaving it.

All depends on being able to see. Frank must be kept wounded. He may lead us to Toma.

                    RICHARD
OK. I am not questioning.

                    MARSILIO
So we understand each other, as before. Yours is the outer and mine the inner. Then we meet in the middle and hold the temple. Capisce?

                    RICHARD
Yes. And Samantha? I am ready to be free of her.

                    MARSILIO
Patience, soon.

                    RICHARD
OK.

                    MARSILIO
Ciao.

MARSILIO hangs up the phone. CLAUDIA gets up and walks over to MARSILIO.

                    CLAUDIA
I have reviewed the protocols for mesmerizing resemblance.

                    MARSILIO
Good. Here is the full compilation on the actress, Rebecca Toma.
        (handing her a flashdrive)
I have tagged the individuating gestures. Memorize them. And remember, it is the feeling. Looks are only to

suggest. Otherwise . . .

CLAUDIA
No chance to incubate a succubus, I know.

MARSILIO
Precisely. Don't act. And avoid being photographed.

CLAUDIA
I know.

INT. BROOKLYN COLLEGE, CLASSROOM – AFTER-
NOON

Projected on the screen are stills from classic 70s horror films:
Zombie, *Suspiria*, *The Exorcist II*, *Don't Look Now*. "To be is
to be cornered – E. M. Cioran, Drawn and Quartered, 1979" is
written on the black board. As FRANK speaks, GARY arrives
outside the open door of the class and waits for the lecture to
finish.

FRANK
. . . so, many things happen in the 70s to transform the
horror genre. Present and premodern fears mix, birthing
scary movies which are more seedy, grim, but also more
artistic and religious. Criminal evil escapes the prison
of murder-mystery and revenge plots, making us see
through the eyes of killer and victim. Supernatural evil
is freed from the gothic frame, making viewers believe
again in the reality of the devil and other medieval su-
perstitions. If the 60s were about love, the spirit of the
70s is fear. Which means they are more horribly real,
more perversely in touch with the dark mystery. As
Cioran says at the end of the decade, "to be is to be cornered." And now *we* are cornered, out of time, so let's
end there.

GARY watches FRANK slowly collect his papers as the students shuffle past him out the door. The students seem less than interested in the class. GARY approaches the desk.

FRANK
Hello. May I help you?

GARY
Professor Mastro, my name is Gary Thatcher. I'm in media studies at NYU, working on cinema and mysticism. I was hoping to talk to you about some of my ideas. I sent you an email a while back.

FRANK
Sorry, I don't remember. What would you like to talk about?

GARY
Well, it's about the last scene of *Forsaken*. I figured it out.

FRANK
Here we go again.

GARY
Will you hear me out?

FRANK
Not if what you are going to say has anything to do with the Illuminati or Knights Templar.

GARY
More like St. Francis's stigmata and the Shroud of Turin.

FRANK

Look, I am sure your speculations are fascinating, but I am not interested. I know what happened. I was there. It was an accident. My cameraman was blinded for Christ's sake!

GARY

You *filmed* your imagination.

FRANK

(pausing)

Maybe I did, maybe I didn't. Either way, it wasn't me, *I* didn't do it. Ever heard the ancient skeptic expression "ou mallon"? I'm with Pyrrho on this: no more.[23]

GARY

Please reconsider, maybe next week? I can prove it, but need a few days. Not something I can send you.

FRANK

Sorry, uh . . . what was your name?

GARY

Gary, Gary Thatcher. And yes, I have heard of Pyrrho, that we should be without opinions, saying about each thing that it no more is than is not. So you cannot deny it.

FRANK

Gary. Right. Like I said. Plus I am going out of town soon.

GARY

Sorry to bother you.

FRANK

It's OK. I am working on something else now.

GARY

OK. Have a nice trip.

GARY walks out, disappointed but calm.

FRANK

Fucking *Forsaken*.

EXT. PARTY AT MAX SLEIMMAN'S HOUSE – NIGHTIME

FRANK enters the party and walks out near the pool where many people are gathered. He looks around, feeling out of place, and eventually sees SAMANTHA, RICHARD, and ROBERT standing near MAX and CAROL SLEIMAN, who are being greeted and congratulated on MAX's new film, *Kingdom of Night*, a thriller set in the Middle East. He walks over to join them, not saying anything until SAMANTHA notices him and moves over with ROBERT to greet him.

SAMANTHA

Frank.

ROBERT

Dad.

FRANK

Congratulations, son. I am proud of you. Samantha. I don't believe it.

RICHARD comes over to join them.

SAMANTHA

It is good to see you. Frank, this is Richard.

RICHARD

Great to finally meet you, Frank.

FRANK

Yes, it's about time.

ROBERT

Let me introduce you to Max Sleiman.

ROBERT leads FRANK over to MAX and CAROL SLEI-MAN. Behind them, near a bar where drinks are being served, is CLAUDIA BRANDINI.

MAX

You have a very talented son.

FRANK

I am happy for his success. And congratulations to you. I never saw that ending coming.

MAX

That was Carol's idea.
    (to Carol)
Carol, this Frank Mastro. Remember the horror movie that gave you all those nightmares back in college? Frank directed it.

FRANK starts to notice CLAUDIA in the distance.

CAROL

Really? I still remember that last scene. Well isn't that funny. Pleased to meet you.

FRANK smiles but appears distracted.

> ROBERT
>
> About the ending, Richard and Max are planning to re-
> lease a personalized version of *The Kingdom* for home
> viewing next year. Plots and scenes will change in real-
> time based on personal history and preferences. The
> movie will never be the same.

> FRANK
>
> That's interesting. Excuse me, but I'm gonna grab a
> drink.

FRANK walks over to the bar near CLAUDIA, who looks at
him and smiles politely. He notices and seems to recognize
something about her. He gets a drink and starts to walk away.
As he does, CLAUDIA walks slowly off in another direction.
FRANK walks away and sits down further off in the garden
by himself. He watches CLAUDIA move through the crowd
and pause near a vase of Narcissus flowers. She gazes into one
of the flowers and touches the petals as if counting them. As
she leans over to examine the flowers, the gold cross around
her neck catches the light and flashes powerfully in FRANK's
eyes. FRANK is subtly dazed and we see his vision widen and
float in a strange way, zooming in on things from a perspective other than his head, conveying a sense of the dissolving of
perspective itself. His vision moves around the scene flashing
through a series of aspects of CLAUDIA's image, as if her
form functions like a dark crystal refracting his awareness in
different directions at once. After the experience builds and
slows, we see FRANK's feet as the camera continues panning
towards his own face, as if he is approaching the threshold of
seeing himself. As the camera gets closer to seeing his face,
someone calls his name. At first the voice is otherworldly, un-
recognizable, but it quickly changes to ROBERT's voice.

ROBERT

How's it going?

FRANK

Oh, good, OK. I was just relaxing for a moment.

ROBERT

See something you like?

FRANK

I don't know.

ROBERT

Anyway, Max asked me to invite you to join him in his study a little later.

FRANK

Alright, thanks.

ROBERT

Let's catch up later, OK?

FRANK

Sure, of course.

ROBERT walks off and FRANK gets up and moves over to CLAUDIA. During the conversation, FRANK perspires.

FRANK

Excuse me, may I ask about your necklace? I happened to notice it flashing in the light earlier.

CLAUDIA

It was talking to you?

FRANK

Perhaps so.

CLAUDIA

It is a very old cross, given to me by my grandmother. Inside is dust of a saint whose name I forget. Precious, no?

FRANK

It is beautiful. You are not Romanian are you?

CLAUDIA

No, Italian. Like you I think?

FRANK

My grandparents were. How did you know?

CLAUDIA

A friend said you are Robert's father. You must be proud?

FRANK

Yes, of course. Not that it is simple.

CLAUDIA

No need to explain. Maybe I understand. A seed flowers without the one who planted it. And this is sorrow and joy.

FRANK

In this case, without *and* despite, and despite without. So yes, you see.

CLAUDIA

Why did you think I was Romanian?

FRANK

An old memory.

CLAUDIA

I am Roman. Is that close enough?

FRANK

Too close, actually.
    (holding out his hand)
I am Frank, Frank Mastro.

CLAUDIA

And I am Emina.

FRANK

Pleased to meet you.
    (shaking hands)

CLAUDIA

Frank, I would like to talk more. Maybe later? But now
Max wants to see me in his study and I can't say no.

FRANK

Then I will go with you. We have the same invitation it
seems.

FRANK and CLAUDIA walk off together, chatting. On their
way back to the house, a maid approaches FRANK and offers
him a towel.

MAID

Sir?

For a moment FRANK is perplexed, but then takes the towel
and wipes his face. CLAUDIA smiles.

FRANK

It is warm here.

CLAUDIA

Yes.

As the MAID walks off, she holds up the towel and looks curiously at the impression of FRANK's sweaty face.

INT. GARY AND ARIANA'S APARTMENT BUILDING – LATE AT NIGHT

GARY sits intently before his computer in a dark room. We see his face, illumined by the light of the screen, from the perspective of the screen. Different colors flash across his face and glasses as we hear the sounds of beheading and other execution videos. He shows no signs of fear or flinching, but looks impassive, calm, serene. There is a subtle glow around the crown of his head, not obvious, but there to be noticed if you think about it.

INT. PARTY AT MAX SLEIMMAN'S HOUSE – NIGHTIME

FRANK and CLAUDIA walk through the house towards MAX's study. In the hallway they meet SAMANTHA, RICHARD, and ROBERT. RICHARD and CLAUDIA accidentally exchange a knowing glance. RICHARD kisses SAMANTHA goodnight.

RICHARD

Goodnight, darling. I'll be home before too long.

SAMANTHA

OK, goodnight.

ROBERT
Frank, I am driving Mom back. Would you like a lift?

FRANK
I think I'll stay a little longer.

RICHARD
I'll drive Frank back.

SAMANTHA
Goodbye, Frank.

FRANK
Goodbye.

INT. GARY AND ARIANA'S APARTMENT BUILDING –
LATE AT NIGHT

GARY sits down kneeling on a traditional Tibetan rug woven
with the image of a flayed man and bordered with severed
heads.[24] He places both of his hands out in front of him on the
carpet, in line with the hands in the image. His feet are together behind him. He leans forward, so that he is on all fours, and
pauses there in stillness, as if ready to be beheaded, and then
touches his forehead to the carpet. He then moves back to a
sitting position, raising his left and right hands as if they are
holding his head and a weapon, respectively. He does this entire motion a total of four times. Each time he touches his head
to the carpet, the perspective of the camera zooms and shifts
in a way to indicate an inversion of perspective through his
head. A simple way to do this would be to shoot the down motion in POV and the return motion from a perspective above
the center of the carpet looking down. This would produce the
sensation of Gary's vision as it were "passing through" the
carpet and popping out above his body after his head is severed by the gesture of bowing.

INT. PARTY AT MAX SLEIMMAN'S HOUSE –
NIGHTIME

MAX, CLAUDIA, RICHARD, and FRANK sit in FRANK's
study in comfortable chairs facing each other in a cross pattern. MAX is at the head position, CLAUDIA at the foot.
RICHARD is to MAX's left and FRANK is to his right. On
the coffee table between them is a replica of The Black Obe-
lisk of Shalmaneser III.[25]

                    RICHARD
But Frank you gotta admit given the way technology is
headed, that the industry needs this. The old models of
aesthetic experience simply don't fit our world any-
more, they don't work. People don't *see* like that today,
they can't.

                    MAX
He's right, Frank.

                    FRANK
Nope. Real cinema deepens vision, reflecting the miracle *that* you are seeing. But this whole immersive neurocinema business, it's about self-absorption, numbness.
That's what I hear when I see a kid in those goggles on
the subway, "Hello, is there anybody in there?"

                    CLAUDIA
Frank is right, from his perspective. But the issue is not
the technology itself, which is inevitable, but the pur-
pose for which a person uses it.

                    FRANK
Or is used by it.

RICHARD

Like Socrates said, even writing produces forgetful-ness.[26] So the question is what you remember in forget-ting, what dreams fill our sleep.

MAX

Take your idea, Frank, for a more spiritual film. Some of the sequencing algorithms Richard's people are working with have the potential to induce psychedelic states. This is the real deal.

FRANK

The fact that you make that equation shows that you re-ally don't see what I am talking about. But we don't need to understand each other. Who is we anyway?

CLAUDIA

Gentlemen, I think it's time to turn this philosophy cir-cle into a spiral. Would anyone care to dance?

RICHARD
Spoken like a true lady.

MAX
You go on ahead, I'll see to the music.

FRANK
I'll dance with you Emina. Not like I have anything to lose.

CLAUDIA winks, gets up and whispers to MAX, who puts on an old Italian song. FRANK and CLAUDIA dance around the room nonchalantly. MAX and RICHARD chat inaudibly about something and look on. As they dance FRANK continues to notice CLAUDIA's cross. CLAUDIA smiles and at one point winks to RICHARD without FRANK or MAX noticing.

CLAUDIA winks at FRANK, causing FRANK to see a kind of flash and image of a face which is like REBECCA TOMA's but also somehow demonic, as with the face similar to AS-TRA's which FRANK saw in the photograph of his tears.

INT. GARY AND ARIANA'S APARTMENT BUILDING – LATE AT NIGHT

GARY, changed into a white shirt, sits before his desk. He calmly and deliberately adjusts a webcam on a small stand and stares into its lens. He then removes a gun from the drawer of his desk and places it on the desk to his right, keeping his hand on it. The camera zooms out, so that we see GARY from behind, with his head blocking our view of the camera he is looking into. He slowly reaches to press record with his left hand and we see the red glow of the recording signal light create an aura around the silhouette of his head.

EXT. LOS ANGELES, RICHARD'S CAR – MIDNIGHT

RICHARD and CLAUDIA are driving FRANK back to his hotel. FRANK sits in the back seat.

RICHARD
Sorry you couldn't stay in town longer, Frank.

FRANK
That's OK, this party will do me for a while.

CLAUDIA
You know, Frank, they might tease you about being idealistic and old fashioned, but I know you are the real thing. The world needs more thrilling divine romance. When I get home, I am going to watch *Forsaken*.

FRANK

Well it is a horror movie, not much romance, not on screen anyway.

CLAUDIA

The best kind.[27]
    (turning around to face him)
It was marvelous to meet you.

FRANK

Yes, it is astonishing, to see you . . .
    (leaning back on the headrest and closing his eyes)
again.

RICHARD sees FRANK close his eyes in the rear view mirror and turns and smiles to CLAUDIA. FRANK remains as if sinking towards sleep while the car speeds through the night. A noise emerges, increasing in volume – the sound of an airplane.

INT/EXT. KENNEDY AIRPORT – EARLY EVENING

FRANK opens his eyes as his airplane lands in JFK Airport. He walks out of baggage to get a taxi. The scene is shot to echo visually the arrival of Suzy Banyon at Munich airport in Argento's *Suspiria*. Where Suzy left from Kennedy airport, FRANK arrives there into a *Suspiria*-esque environment: colored lighting, woman in red, rain and wind, creepy automatic doors [cinematic decapitation motif], laconic cabbie, etc. This is done to suggest the idea of a fluid interface between cinema and reality, and with it FRANK's departure from his routine life.

INT. FRANK MASTRO'S APARTMENT – NIGHT

FRANK gets home, pours himself a whiskey, and puts *For-*

saken on to watch. We see the opening shot with title, then he fast-forwards to the final scene. In *Forsaken*'s final shot, the Satanic witch Cinnaedea, played by REBECCA TOMA, in order to gain immortal life, decapitates herself with a sword, spurting blood into the mouths of two young acolytes and her own severed head. Then, as her attendants whisper strange hymns, Cinnaedea's body slowly becomes young again, picks up its head, and walks away. We watch FRANK watch the scene from behind his head, noticing his subtle reactive movements stimulated by some hidden memories of the event. The scene is shot in a forest at dawn, producing fluctuations in light as bodies move in front of the sun. But there is at least one other subtle flash on the film which occurs at the moment of decapitation. FRANK re-examines the scene, pausing and replaying certain frames. Each time he sees certain moments, his face and neck and left arm flinch and/or twitch, indicating the presence of some kind of deep *psychic tethering* to the images, as if his present vision is wired to that scene but some kind of subtle *imaginal nerve*. This fascinates but also freaks him out, drawing him back to Gary's notion that he filmed his imagination. That is, just as he filmed his imagination, the film image is like a sensitive extension of his body. Exhausted, he falls asleep amid a montage of memories of the opening "dream" sequence, *Forsaken*, and his recent experiences in L.A.

INT. CHURCH IN BROOKLYN, NY – PREDAWN

Very close close-up of SISTER CONNELLY alone at her morning prayers. Her head covering is worn low on her forehead. There are indications that she is in a state of ecstasy. Her pose is very still. Her eyes are half closed, watery, and partially back in her head. Her mouth is slightly open and silently sighing. She finishes her prayers and returns to a more normal state. She places her rosary in her pocket and takes out a handkerchief, with which she very discreetly wipes the pew in a few places. Putting her handkerchief away, which looks stained, she gets up and walks away, pulling her sleeves down over her hands as she goes.

INT. FRANK MASTRO'S APARTMENT – DAWN

He wakes right before dawn, sees the time on the alarm clock, 4:20 AM, and then falls back to sleep. Very slowly, a young REBECCA TOMA, wearing Jordache jeans[28] and a t-shirt with no bra, walks into his bedroom and sits on the bed next to him, placing her hand on his head. He wakes and she lays on top of him. They gaze into each other's eyes and REBECCA's eyes fill with tears. Slowly she starts to cry and sob, dripping tears onto Frank's face. As he begins to taste and open his mouth to catch her tears, her sobbing becomes more sensual and she presses her body onto him as if sexually aroused. Tears and saliva drip from her face in slow rapture. The fluid fills FRANK's mouth and he begins to be unable to breathe. As REBECCA gazes into him, FRANK seems paralyzed, unable to move, as per the classic astral presentation of the incubus/succubus.[29] He breaks the spell and wakes in his bedroom at 6:00 am, staring into space.

INT/EXT. MAUSOLEUM – EARLY MORNING

CLAUDIA and ROBERT sit together inside a pyramidal mausoleum. RICHARD's clothes are placed on a small altar at the back of the chamber, next to which are steps leading down to a crypt of some kind. There is a sound of running water. Semi-verbal sighs and moans, of pain and pleasure, echo from below, along with the pulse of a strobe light.

CLAUDIA
There is nothing to fear. She gives nothing but your own self.

ROBERT
What am I to do?

CLAUDIA
Only whatever comes natural. As you please.

ROBERT
And afterwards?

CLAUDIA
You will feel new strength, more life. No one else will know.

ROBERT
May I have the record?

CLAUDIA
No. Signor Barbi will do the reading. In later years he may teach you. Now you must only listen, carefully.

ROBERT
OK.

CLAUDIA
And beware the desire to return here. It will feel over-powering, but you would lose double what you gain. To open the Sibyl without the key is forbidden.

The sounds and lights from below cease and RICHARD re-turns to CLAUDIA, handing her a large crystal key. He is na-ked, sweaty, with some signs of blood and marks on his body. CLAUDIA looks to ROBERT, who then disrobes. CLAUDIA hands ROBERT the key.

CLAUDIA
Seven minutes.

INT. CONVENT IN BROOKLYN, NY – EARLY MORN-ING[30]

SISTER CONNELLY sits at the small desk in her private room. She picks up a small knife and carefully scrapes black-ish dried blood from a handkerchief onto a piece of paper, which she then examines under a magnifying glass. Folding the piece of paper, she guides the blood-dust into a glass bottle which is already half full and tucks it away in her garments.

INT. COLLEGE, FRANK MASTRO'S CLASS – LATE MORNING

As class lets out, two men, DETECTIVES LAND and RAMIREZ, approach FRANK's desk.

DETECTIVE LAND
Professor Mastro?

FRANK
Yes?

DETECTIVE LAND
I am Detective Land and this is Detective Ramirez. We would like to ask you a few questions, if that's alright with you.

FRANK
Is everything OK?

DETECTIVE LAND
Well, that's what we are trying to figure out. Do you know a person by the name of Gary Thatcher?

FRANK
I met him last week. He approached me after class,

wanted to talk to me about his research, in media studies.

DETECTIVE LAND

I see.

DETECTIVE RAMIREZ

Do you know where he is now?

FRANK

No. I left him a message early this morning and was hoping to meet with him today.

DETECTIVE LAND

Yes, we heard that message. What did you mean that "something strange happened?"

FRANK

Oh, I was referring to an experience I had, which I thought he would be interested in.

DETECTIVE RAMIREZ

Could you be more specific?

FRANK

Well it is not very easy to explain, more of a . . . spiritual experience.

DETECTIVE LAND

I see. Can you tell us where you were as of last Friday?

FRANK

Sure, I was in Los Angeles to attend a movie opening. I left Friday and I got into Kennedy last night.

RAMIREZ whispers to LAND

DETECTIVE LAND

Professor, those are all the questions we have for you today. If you should hear from Gary Thatcher, please let us know immediately. Here is my card. He has disappeared under unusual circumstances.

FRANK

What do you mean?

DETECTIVE RAMIREZ

We are not at liberty to discuss the details with you. Is there a number where we can reach you if necessary?

FRANK

Here is my cell number.

He writes the number down on the top of a piece of scrap paper with the photocopy of an image on the other side, tears the paper, and hands it to the detectives.

DETECTIVE LAND

Thank you.

The detectives exit and Frank looks at the torn sheet of paper, turning it over to see what was on the other side. It is the picture of a 70s horror actress, like Madeline Smith, posing with a bicycle. He has torn the head off.

EXT. OUTSIDE FRANK'S COLLEGE – MIDDAY

On the street, as FRANK is exiting campus, ARIANA FOX calls out and runs up to him.

ARIANA

Professor Mastro?

FRANK

Yes.

ARIANA

My name is Ariana. I am Gary's girlfriend, Gary Thatcher. Did the police speak with you?

FRANK

Yes, earlier today.

ARIANA

Oh, good. I don't know what to do. I am really worried, but can't imagine that Gary would kill himself.

FRANK

Kill himself?

ARIANA

The detectives showed you the video right?

FRANK

No, what video?

ARIANA

I thought they were going to show you. Gary made it, for you. OK, we need to talk. Can you come to our apartment? Maybe you can help me figure out where he is.

FRANK

OK.

EXT/INT. ARIANA AND GARY'S APARTMENT BUILD-ING

They arrive at Gary and Ariana's apartment. ARIANA shows

FRANK Gary's desk.

                    ARIANA
        Can I get you a drink or something?
            (she lights a cigarette)
        Sorry but I am little over the edge right now.

                    FRANK
        Sit down and tell me what happened.

They sit.

                    ARIANA
        When I came home late at night on Friday, Gary wasn't
        here. I called everyone, but his phone is here and no-
        body has seen him. Next morning I find the video, freak
        out, and call the police.

                    FRANK
        Can I see the video?

                    ARIANA
        It's on his computer. The file is named "Forsake Me."
        It's awful. But first I have to tell you that it can't be re-
        al. Even though it looks . . . too real.

Frank gets the laptop, places it on the coffee table, and we get
to watch it as if sitting between FRANK and ARIANA. In the
video, GARY is sitting before his computer screen. He says,
"Alright, let's try this again. Frank Mastro, this is for you, for
Forsaken. You showed me the way!" Gary then picks up a
gun, winks at the camera, and shoots himself in the head. We
see the spray of blood, the body collapses, and then the clip
ends. FRANK winces, pours himself a drink.

ARIANA

The police were all over the place and they couldn't
find any trace of blood, and no gun. It's like what he
shot *only happened on the video*.

FRANK

I don't understand. Maybe he just faked it. Special effects.

ARIANA

That's what the cops said. It was uploaded early Friday
morning to a pseudocide forum.

FRANK

Pseudocide forum?

ARIANA

Yeah, a website where people post fake suicide videos.
Gary showed me some a while ago. Some are not. So-
cial media gone *memento mori* in a sick way.

FRANK

The more we represent ourselves, the more we want to
kill ourselves. I get it. So that proves he is OK, if he uploaded the video.

ARIANA

But there are no signs of editing. The video is coded as
recorded with a timer. And Gary is not here, I just don't
get it.

FRANK

Like he survived his own suicide by disappearing. That
is mad. There must be an explanation.

ARIANA

You tell me! Gary is obsessed with your film. He must have done what he said you did.

FRANK

Let's take a step back. Can you tell me about his research?

ARIANA

He's studying premodern theories of the imagination and the cinematic nature of consciousness. Like the idea of seeing your whole life flash before your eyes at death. That goes way back.

FRANK

Interesting. Are you in school too?

ARIANA

No, more of a lost poet, unfinished auto-documentary. Gary and I met in Rome last summer when he was on fellowship. What an adventure that was, is. Total "al di lá."

FRANK

I can imagine. So how does *Forsaken* fit in?

ARIANA

Forsäkken. Gary likes to say like that, as if it were a black metal band, which it also is.

FRANK

Truth stranger than truth.

ARIANA

He is a huge horror fan, since he was little, always fascinated by the spectacle of death. That led to mysticism,

Georges Bataille and so forth. It's the idea of martyr-dom he's into. No seeing without dying.

FRANK

I understand. The eye of death and the death of the I. That's what I wanted to channel in *Forsaken*, through the eyes of the saints.

ARIANA

Well you certainly channeled *something*.

FRANK

And I still can't shake the damned thing. It's like the Pope's murder cursed the film into believing in me with a faith I couldn't live with.

ARIANA

On his seventh birthday Gary's parents—God knows why—let him watch *The Exorcist*. He calls it his 'first communion'. Says it was like a hidden switch flipped in his mind and horror flicks were never frightening again because he knew they *were real*. I think he is searching for something to put the fear back in him.

FRANK

Mind if I look around his desk?

ARIANA

Please. There's some gory stuff there. Gary is fearless that way. Watches all the beheading videos without moving a muscle. Stiller than fucking Sir Gawain.

FRANK looks around Gary's desk. There is a bulletin board with a constellation of items which the camera pans through: the print-out of a newspaper headline for the death of Pope John Paul I in 1978, the film poster for *Forsaken*, an article about P2 (Propaganda Due), an etching of Plato's Allegory of the Cave, the Templecombe Head,[31] a painting of the Veronica, photograph of the Shroud of Turin,[32] a painting of St. Denis picking up his own head,[33] a recent article about Oculus Media and neurocinema research, a screenshot of the beheading scene from *The Omen* (1976),[34] detail of the medieval image of the beheading of St. Albans (showing the headsman's eyes popping out),[35] a colored diagram for visualizing four dimensions from Charles Howard Hinton's *The Fourth Dimension* (1904),[36] a renaissance engraving of Narcissus before his reflection, various pictures of stigmatics, a Chinese beheading photograph, and at the center of them all, the Chinnamasta icon.[37] Next to that is a page from the *Spiritual Exercises* of Ignatius of Loyola, showing the diagram of a hand.[38] FRANK reaches out instinctively to touch it, and we see a flash of the moment of the opening vision of the Pope's murder when one of the THREE FIGURES places the parchment in his side. On the desk are a variety of esoteric, horror, and conspiracy theory books: David Yallop's *In God's Name*, Bonaventure's *Journey of the Mind into God*, Peter Levenda's *Sinister Forces*, Douglas Harding's *On Having No Head*,[39] Ramsey Campbell's *The Nameless*,[40] etc.

FRANK

Has Gary been talking to anyone else recently about his research? A lot of this stuff seems rather outside the realm of media studies.

ARIANA

Just to me, and to his advisor, Thomas Berg. He doesn't really hang out with other people that much. Oh, and Sister Connelly, a nun in Brooklyn. She wrote the book there on the right, *As a Seal Upon Thy Heart*.

We see the book title and cover, showing an image of the five wounds of Christ, a bleeding sacred heart in the middle, with an eye in its center.[41]

Gary met with her several times last month, right after we came back from Rome. The book tries to explain the stigmata miracle scientifically, how in ecstasy the mind can imprint a body with its vision.

FRANK
I know this is really hard, Ariana. But the video looks real. Maybe Gary wanted out and had an accomplice, to spare you finding his body. I have heard of people doing that.

ARIANA
That's impossible. Gary wouldn't! There is no note or message. And in the video he is trying it again, like it's a stunt.

FRANK
Well he must be somewhere.

ARIANA
That is why I came to you. He is not dead and I need to find out what is going on.

FRANK
OK, right. I have to admit that this is not the first inexplicable thing I have witnessed in my life.

They sit in silence for a little while, long enough for the viewer to feel uncomfortable, generating a sense of the uncanny presence of the world to itself.

FRANK
What are you doing tomorrow? Maybe we could talk to Sister Connelly.

                    ARIANA
I will try to make an appointment.

                    FRANK
I also want to understand what Gary knows.

                    ARIANA
Yes, I can see that.

EXT/INT. MOUNTAIN LODGE, NEW HAMPSHIRE –
PRE-DAWN

Shot from afar, showing mountain landscape, then zooming in.
Upstairs the revelry of a group of young professionals is running out of steam in a luxury bar room. Downstairs, in a small
basement room, GARY THATCHER is being startled awake
by glaring lights and loud discordant music in the small room
where he is being held against his will. After half a minute or
so of the sleep-depriving torture, TWO MEN in black ski
masks enter the room with a cappuccino and pastry, standing
there as he slowly eats and drinks. One of the TWO MEN
walks outside to turn the music off, then returns. Gary finishes
the breakfast and looks up at them.

EXT. BROOKLYN STREET – MIDDAY

FRANK and ARIANA walking to meet Sister Connelly.

                    FRANK
What did Gary tell you about his meetings with Sister
Connelly.

                    ARIANA
Not much. But I get the feeling their conversations were
intense. He was always quiet, withdrawn afterwards in a
weird way.

                    FRANK
How did he meet her?

                    ARIANA
Through her book, which he found in Rome. Seems it
was pretty controversial, in 1987, the Church not liking
having its mysteries explained and all.

                    FRANK
1987?

                    ARIANA
Yes, why?

                    FRANK
Oh, nothing, an old memory. Like the whole autopsy
question surrounding the Pope's body in '78. Some
things you just don't pry into.

INT. MOUNTAIN LODGE, NEW HAMPSHIRE – EARLY
MORNING

The TWO MEN place a hood over his head, restrain his hands
with a plastic tie, and lead him to another room with a desk.
On the other side of the desk sits MARSILIO BARBI, wearing a green suit.

                    MARSILIO
Buon giorno, Gary. I hope the cappuccino was to your
tastes.

                    GARY
Yes, it was delicious.

                    MARSILIO
So, what would you like to tell us today?

                    GARY

I can talk about my dissertation, the chapter on Bonaventure. I bet you have even heard of Bonaventure.

                    MARSILIO

Bonaventura da Bagnoregio, of course. I have also seen
your article on the Franciscan concept of the phantasm
in the *Journal of Consciousness Studies*. Impressive.[42]

                    GARY

Precisely.

                    MARSILIO

Being clever won't help you here. Eventually you tell
us what we want to know. There will be no choice.

                    GARY

And what is that? Please tell me, so I can tell you, and
we can get out of here.

                    MARSILIO

Let me refresh your memory.

INT/EXT. CONVENT IN BROOKLYN – MIDDAY

SISTER CONNELLY sits in her room, wrapped in a blue
shawl, staring catatonically into space. A NUN knocks on the
door and pokes her head in the room.

                    NUN

Sister Connelly. There are two people outside in the
garden waiting to see you.
        (after the lack of a response)
Sister Connelly?

SISTER CONNELLY
I am coming.

SISTER CONNELLY walks out to the grounds in the back of the convent, where she finds FRANK and ARIANA sitting on benches waiting for her. She walks up to them, but does not say anything.

ARIANA
Sister Connelly?

SISTER CONNELLY looks at FRANK and ARIANA as if scrutinizing them, maybe reading their minds. FRANK and ARIANA look puzzled. After a few moments SISTER CONNELLY nods and almost smiles.

ARIANA
Sister Connelly, I am Ariana. And this is Frank, Frank Mastro. How are you today?

SISTER CONNELLY
Hello Ariana. Aryan, noble. I am Sister Connelly. Conghal, wolf-fierce. And about Gary, he is OK. Do not worry.

ARIANA
He is? How do you know? Thank God.

SISTER CONNELLY
Anything else?

FRANK
Sister, do you know where Gary is?

SISTER CONNELLY starts to drift away into the garden. FRANK and ARIANA follow.

SISTER CONNELLY
Gary, gar, spear . . . He is one who . . .

BEGIN FLASHBACK – SERIES OF SHOTS:

A) GARY and SISTER CONNELLY sitting in the common area of the convent.

B) GARY and SISTER CONNELLY walking in the convent grounds.

C) SISTER CONNELLY placing her hands on GARY's head.

D) GARY swooning to the ground and shaking as SISTER CONNELLY prays her rosary in the background.

E) SISTER CONNELLY leading GARY back to the church.

F) GARY alone in the church. He prays, crosses himself, and then removes a small phial containing a blackish powder, which he pours into his mouth.

SISTER CONNELLY (V.O.) (cont'd)
. . . how can I say? Everything true is clouded. Knowledge is nothing. I used to think . . . Now no question makes sense. Not one. Gary wanted answers. But the wounds are only five. He is learning to count. I have done my duty. *Secretum meum mihi*, my secret to myself.

SISTER CONNELLY stops walking and stares at FRANK.

SISTER CONNELLY
Yes?

FRANK
Secret? What do you mean?

                    SISTER CONNELLY
Secret, you know, sacred, something set apart, severed.
Like the Indian saints who dismember themselves at
will.[43] What is one in four dimensions looks separated
in three.[44]

                    ARIANA
Sister, please, I must find Gary. If you know anything
that might help, tell us.

                    SISTER CONNELLY
Information is zero, zero, and zero. Remember what the
dead abbess used to tell me? To find you must follow.
To follow you must see. To see you must look. To look
you must search . . . where he is – your heart.

FRANK, who has been staring at SISTER CONNELLY begins to feel a little faint. He moves over to a bench as ARIA-
NA reaches to help him. SISTER CONNELLY comes over
and sits between them.

                    SISTER CONNELLY
Frank, Francis, free, frank. I don't think this one can
keep a secret!

                    FRANK
I'm OK, just a little tired.

                    SISTER CONNELLY
I am too.

SISTER CONNELLY places her hands on the side of
FRANK's head and looks into his eyes, then more intensely,
as if gazing at something far away. FRANK closes his eyes,
then she closes hers. We zoom in to SISTER CONNELLY'S
face and eyes, through the middle of her forehead, then into

the star-filled blackness of her skull.

EXT. DESERT IN SYRIA DESERT – MIDDAY

Two TEMPLAR KNIGHTS ride side by side on horses through a desert landscape. They are tired and haggard. The KNIGHT on the left speaks first.

> LEFT TEMPLAR
> The order is lost. It is time to seek protection of the secret from the Five, at the White Castle.

> RIGHT TEMPLAR
> We must not! No one knows what might become of it. Their charge is black, beyond discernment.

> LEFT TEMPLAR
> Yes, but only thus will the truth be *saved*.

> RIGHT TEMPLAR
> I fear what they are capable of. It will be our damnation!

> LEFT TEMPLAR
> Salvation? I do not care for it. Our city is Roma, Amor, the Eternal City! And Paul says to the Romans, "I have great sorrow and unceasing anguish in my heart. For I wish that I myself were accursed and cut off from Christ for the sake of my brethren."

> RIGHT TEMPLAR
> You are right. There is no greater love.[45]

The camera pans into the blue sky. The blue sky fades into the blue of SISTER CONNELLY's habit. The camera moves at close range along SISTER CONNELLY's arms and towards her hands which she is still holding on FRANK's temples. The camera passes through the back of SISTER CONNELLY's left hand and enters the blackness of FRANK's head, wherein a play of colors, similar to the flames flickering over the corpses in the opening scene, begin to appear.

EXT/INT. A CASTLE IN A DESERT LANDSCAPE – SUNSET

The TEMPLAR KNIGHTS arrive before a square castle resembling Chastel Blanc in Safita, Syria,[46] but considerably smaller, more like a shrine. It looks to be the same as the one in the opening scene. The entrance is flanked by two large columns, capped with large stone spheres. They dismount and stand gazing at it. A young BOY sits on the front steps, playing with an azure ball. He stands and approaches the knights.

> RIGHT TEMPLAR
> Tell your master that we seek protection of the essence of our Order.

The BOY walks into the castle, then returns.

> BOY
> Master says, "The salt of your life will not flow to the sea, the dust of the Order will not be scattered, the head of your Head shall never die."[47] Follow me and make the offering. Enter by the only way.

The BOY enters the castle. The TEMPLARS embrace, give each other the kiss of peace, and unsheathe their swords.

> RIGHT AND LEFT TEMPLAR
> (in unison and grasping each other's arms)
> *Nesciat sinistra tua quid faciat dextera tua.*

The LEFT TEMPLAR gets on his knees and bows his head forward with arms outstretched towards the east. The RIGHT TEMPLAR beheads him. As the head falls, the LEFT TEM-PLAR catches it in his hands, showing us the reflection of the sun in its eyes. Then, the LEFT TEMPLAR stands and the RIGHT TEMPLAR kneels facing the west. The LEFT TEM-PLAR, holding his head in his left hand, decapitates the RIGHT TEMPLAR. The RIGHT TEMPLAR catches his head and stands facing the sun. The TEMPLAR KNIGHTS enter the castle side by side, holding hands and their severed heads.[48] We see the outline of one of the FIVE FIGURES be-hind an altar and the TEMPLARS kneeling to offer their heads as the screen becomes brilliant with light and sound.

EXT. CONVENT IN BROOKLYN – MIDDAY

SISTER CONNELLY swoons, gazing upward with a sigh and releasing FRANK's head as ARIANA holds her.

ARIANA
Sister, are you OK?

SISTER CONNELLY
Yes, dear.

SISTER CONNELLY reaches for a handkerchief to wipe the sweat from FRANK's brow. FRANK looks dazed. As she does so we see that there are a few small drops of blood, where her hands had been, among the beads of sweat which she wipes away inconspicuously.

ARIANA
What were you doing?

SISTER CONNELLY
Listening.

ARIANA

Frank, are you OK?

FRANK

Yes. Just felt a little faint that's all. Then for some reason, when I closed my eyes, it seemed that I was home, not here. Did I fall asleep?

ARIANA

No, we've just been sitting and conversing.

FRANK

I don't understand . . . half remember something. A dream, except that I was neither dreaming nor in it. Like a movie.

SISTER CONNELLY

Did you see something?

FRANK

I don't know. What were we talking about? I feel, I don't know . . . like I died when it stopped.

ARIANA

When what stopped?

FRANK and SISTER CONNELLY

(simultaneously)

I don't know.

A NUN from the convent approaches.

NUN

Sister Connelly, you are asked for in the refectory.

SISTER CONNELLY nods slowly and the NUN walks away.

SISTER CONNELLY

To see headlessly, with the eye of heart, walking in that spiral sphere, what is there to say? It is like a fourth dimension. Wound of everything, never healing.

ARIANA

Please, before you go, is there anything you can tell us about Gary. I am so worried. It is not like him to disappear like this.

SISTER CONNELLY stands up.

SISTER CONNELLY

And to appear? There is no one to worry about.

FRANK

What did you mean that Gary is learning to count?

SISTER CONNELLY

The fire he has swallowed is perilous, beyond control. Perilous, from per, to risk, try. He must now ex*per*ience.

ARIANA and FRANK stand up. ARIANA kisses SISTER CONNELLY's hands.

ARIANA

Pray for him.

SISTER CONNELLY

All shall be well.[49] This is only shadow, a reflection, the speculation of Whoever is looking into it.
  (taking her necklace and placing it over ARIANA's head)
From speculare, to look into a mirror.

ARIANA
What is this?

ARIANA opens the small pendant on the necklace and sees that it contains a negative image of the face from the Shroud of Turin.

SISTER CONNELLY
A trinket, a trick, from *tricari*, to be evasive – 'tis an image trapped once in the darkroom of a heart.

ARIANA
Thank you. I will keep it, for Gary.

SISTER CONNELLY
I would say that it will protect you, but who needs that? Go in peace.

SISTER CONNELLY turns and exits as a siren sounds in the near distance.

INT. MOUNTAIN LODGE, NEW HAMPSHIRE – EARLY MORNING

Begin with a moment of taut silence during which MARSILIO stares fiercely at GARY, who is still hooded.

MARSILIO
(becoming increasingly menacing)
Dio bono! You think we don't know what happened? You have no idea who you are dealing with. The Holy Father dies of a "heart attack." *Forsaken*'s final scene is filmed, with uncanny mastery on the same night, the very hour! Thirty-nine years later, Mastro-fanboy here visits the Vatican Library to examine marginalia in the Pope's copy of the *Spiritual Exercises*, a unique edition,

translated into Italian not from Ignatius's original but from the much expanded Cypriot Maronite Arabic version.[50] See, I know my shit! Three weeks later, the brilliant student does something most dumb. Posts a suicide video to an internet forum, a video bearing how shall we say, certain unmistakable *signatures* which only another party can recognize. How do you think we found you? Now stop lying and tell us how the fuck you made that video!

(pulling off Gary's hood)

GARY

I don't know. It is not possible to explain how.

MARSILIO

You mean how you *did* it. So you admit to knowing the secret.

GARY

My secret to myself, woe is me. So fuck off! I can't tell you anything, nothing.

MARSILIO

We will bring it to the surface. There is nothing which the human tongue, or brain, cannot tell.

GARY

Obviously you don't know shit, whoever you think you are.

MARSILIO

I am a man in green. That is all you will know. Take twenty-four hours to think on your sins and change your mind. After that, the pain begins. And there is no greater pain than seeing your love suffer.

EXT. MANHATTAN BRIDGE – AFTERNOON

FRANK and ARIANA walk slowly across the bridge towards Manhattan.

> ARIANA
> Are you OK?

> FRANK
> I don't know. I feel strange.

> ARIANA
> Strange how?

> FRANK
> I don't know. Anything I say will be wrong.

> ARIANA
> Well say anything and let it be wrong. The whole world is.

> FRANK
> You said it. I feel totally relieved and like garbage at the same time. I'd jump off the bridge now, were I not so afraid that I would fly.

> ARIANA
> To have never wanted less to want anything.

> FRANK
> To have wasted your entire life, until now. The moment everyone seeks and fears, knowing that it never stops happening. If you don't see *that*, you haven't seen anything.

ARIANA
Death by individuation?[51]

FRANK
Maybe salvation is no one to save.[52]

ARIANA
Do you believe what Sister Connelly says is true?

FRANK
It doesn't matter.

ARIANA
Whether you believe or whether it is true?

FRANK
Both. But we will find Gary, don't worry.

ARIANA
What is the matter with everything?

FRANK
Nothing. Nothing at all. That's the problem.

FRANK and ARIANA arrive at the center of the bridge. They look out toward the Brooklyn Bridge and see a sailboat nearby drifting dead in the water. Some police boats are approaching it. This should evoke, but not directly refer to, the opening scene in Lucio Fulci's *Zombie* (1979).[53]

ARIANA
Seems that something is the matter with that boat down there.

FRANK
There is no one on it.

> (pause)
> Last time I walked across that bridge was with Astra.

They begin walking again, noticing a MAN in the distance who seems to be following them.

> ARIANA
> Is that man following us?

> FRANK
> No, I don't think so.
> (pause)
> We played a counting game stepping on the wooden slats. She called it Peak-a-Byss.

> ARIANA
> Smart cookie. How did she die?

> FRANK
> In 1987, three days after her mother came to live with us.

> ARIANA
> She was the actress in *Forsaken*?

> FRANK
> Yes.

BEGIN FLASHBACK:

EXT. MANHATTAN STREET – DAYTIME

ASTRA walks with FRANK and REBECCA on a busy Manhattan street in 1987. The scene is shot around the child's perspective, with the heads of FRANK and REBECCA out of frame, virtually beheaded. FRANK produces a bouquet of

Narcissus flowers from behind his back for REBECCA.

> FRANK

For you!

> REBECCA

Narcissus! My favorite. I can't believe it. That I am really here, that we are here. I love New York. I love you!

> FRANK

What to say? I love you too. Everything is going to work now, I feel it. She is so happy.

> REBECCA

I know. And you, "Doctor" Mastro, where will you take me tonight?

> FRANK

Anywhere.

INT. CAB OF A TRUCK ON A MANHATTAN STREET – DAYTIME
Two men, DRIVER and PASSENGER, drive down a Manhattan avenue.

> PASSENGER

Man, what is it with you and directions?

> DRIVER

Nothing. I was right back there. This *is* the way.

> PASSENGER

Right.

EXT. MANHATTAN STREET – DAYTIME

ASTRA

Look Dad! Mom look!
   (ASTRA slows and starts to point back behind her)

REBECCA

   (noticing an advertisement on a passing bus)
How about Windows on the World?[54]

FRANK

Super. We will go to the new room, Cellar in the Sky.
   (winks)

REBECCA

Perfect!
   (winks)

ASTRA

Look! Look at that man. He is not wearing any shoes.

ASTRA falls behind FRANK and REBECCA as they begin to enter a crosswalk, absorbed in their own conversation. ASTRA hangs back to look at something behind her. FRANK and REBECCA keep walking forward out of the frame. ASTRA turns around to look for her parents and then dashes into the crosswalk to catch up with them.

INT. CAB OF A TRUCK ON A MANHATTAN STREET – DAYTIME

PASSENGER

OK, at the next street, turn left.

DRIVER

It's one-way the wrong way. I am going straight.

                         PASSESENGER
It doesn't matter. Do you see the traffic ahead? Turn
right!

                         DRIVER
OK, taking it, pulling right.

The DRIVER makes a quick turn right through the intersection.

EXT. CROSSWALK – DAYTIME

ASTRA is killed by the truck as she rushes forward through
the crosswalk, stepping only on the white paint. We see her
hair spread out on the street from under the wheel that comes
to a sudden stop on her crushed skull. REBECCA and
FRANK hear a scream and turn around from the other end of
the crosswalk and we see them run forward, this time showing
the backs of their heads, but not their faces. REBECCA collapses near ASTRA's corpse and FRANK falls to his knees in
shock.

END FLASHBACK.

EXT. MANHATTAN BRIDGE – AFTERNOON

FRANK and ARIANA coming to the end of the bridge in Chi-
natown.

                         ARIANA
God, I am so sorry.

                         FRANK
What to say?

INT. CONVENT IN BROOKLYN – EARLY EVENING

SISTER CONNELLY moves restlessly around her room and then falls to the floor. Then she sits up, weeping and rocking her body. She removes the veil from her head, revealing a star-like scab in the middle of her forehead.[55] The weeping and rocking intensifies, until she begins to bang her forehead on the floor, beneath the crucifix in her room, where a stone protrudes from the floor a little above the others. She bangs her head a total of seven times. With the first thud, we see a flash of a black pyramid. With the second thud, we enter the interior of the pyramid, as shown in the opening scene, with a pattern of dots of light projected on its sides. With the third thud, the projection shifts to show the beheaded TEMPLAR KNIGHTS entering the white shrine/castle. With the fourth thud, the projection shifts, with a flash of patterned dots, to show the beheading by guillotine of King Louis XVI, with a man (as per the legend) raising the head and shouting, "Jacques de Molay, thou art avenged!"[56] With the fifth thud, the projection shifts, with a flash of patterned dots, to show the first kinetoscope images by Thomas Edison, in which the splicing of the frames produces deformations of the figures suggestive of decapitation.[57] With the sixth thud, the projection shifts, with a flash of patterned dots, to show the blinding of Frank's cameraman Sol while shooting the final scene of *Forsaken*. With the seventh thud, we see a suicide bomber detonate himself near the entrance to a small white Sufi shrine with traditional green trim. As his severed head lands on the ground, SISTER CONNELLEY falls silent, stops her headbanging, wipes the blood from her forehead, replaces her head scarf, and lies down on her bed.

INT. MOUNTAIN LODGE, NEW HAMPSHIRE – EARLY EVENING

GARY sits restrained in a high-tech torture chair with robotic attachments and sensors. He has an Oculus mask on his face. CLAUDIA BRANDINI removes the mask, which is wet with tears. GARY looks bewildered. CLAUDIA exits the basement room, walks up a spiral staircase, and enters an office where MARSILIO BARBI stands.

CLAUDIA

Signor Barbi, the observation is finished. As anticipated, his response to the *Forsaken* sequence was deep. But the pattern analysis shows . . . well, look for yourself.

(she hands MARSILIO a tablet)

MARSILIO

I do not understand. This indicates a radical *anticorrelation*. You have parametrized for all sequencings of the first 39 primes, discounting 2 and 3?

CLAUDIA

Yes, of course, as well as cross-checked for patterning between twins and non-twins.

MARSILIO

But . . .

CLAUDIA

Yes, the degree of invariance is unmatched even by Cotard delusion.[58]

MARSILIO

Impossible, but not unforeseen. His secret keeps its secret by means of the secret itself, by cutting himself off from itself. And the internet traffic statistics?

CLAUDIA

The non-random spike in *Forsaken* access is steady since Sunday night.

MARSILIO

Good. Your succubus is strong. There will now be an increase, then a dip before it peaks. So we must watch carefully, in order not to miss the resonance phase.

CLAUDIA

Sorry, I do not understand.

MARSILIO

Images are threads of the invisible. Some go all the way to the Outside, like the radii of a spider web. Through a person for whom the thread is vital, it can be struck, like the string of a harp. This attracts others. But if the image is caused to resonate, this calls the spider, the principle which first created it. And we, my beautiful, are the spider hunter!

CLAUDIA

How will we know if the "spider," as you call it, is called?

MARSILIO

It is not easy to say. Something will appear, a presence that no one should see. And whatever that is, it will hold a key for unlocking the secret.

CLAUDIA

I will monitor the traffic and ready the chamber.

MARSILIO

Good. Next we must overlay the *Forsaken* sequence through a pain-matrix with the cross impressions in order to accelerate the amygdala.

CLAUDIA

I understand. And sir, the candidates await you in the conference room.

MARSILIO

Of course.

MARSILIO walks out of his office into a meeting room with a long table where about a dozen CANDIDATES are gathered, dressed identically in corporate attire. In front of each of them, on a small silver saucer, is a tiny black confection in the shape of a pyramid.

MARSILIO

Ladies and gentlemen. It has been a pleasure to spend this wondrous week with you. None of you would be here if you did not have something very unique to offer the world. As life becomes ever more penetrated by virtual experience, it is essential, for the future of humanity itself, to ensure the humanness of that experience. This is our task: to personalize reality, to make it ours, all the way down.[59] No longer only spectators in this universe, we are becoming its creators, the dreamers of the world. To confirm and celebrate your commitment to this great work, we have prepared a special festivity, a dream masquerade! Before you is the pane-seme-serpente, the serpent-seed bread, a lozenge of ancient recipe which will hold your silver gate ajar for six hours without sleep. Wake and dream wisely! None will remember nor forget tonight's experiences, which will never die, but burn forever like an invisible fire, brightening the fringes of reality's film. Now dissolve the serpent into your tongue and follow me.

All place the lozenges on their tongues and MARSILIO leads the CANDIDATES outside where they wander towards a grove with some fires burning in the distance.

INT. FRANK MASTRO'S APARTMENT – EVENING

FRANK and ARIANA are sitting in the living room. Some papers, books, and a bottle of wine are spread out before them.

ARIANA

Assuming Gary did uncover something dangerous about 1978, where might he have gone, and who might have taken him?

FRANK

Who knows, there are conspiracy theories.

ARIANA

What do you think happened? You were there.

FRANK

I never really believed any of the explanations.

ARIANA

Why not?

FRANK

Blind intuition I guess. And there's a dream I've had. I see the Pope killed, crucified upside down like St. Peter, and then decapitated.

ARIANA

Holy fuck. That is some dream. What if it actually happened?

FRANK

I had the dream the morning Gary came to my class.

ARIANA

What?

FRANK

Yeah, feels like I'm walking into a guillotine of total co-incidence, an empyrean conspiracy. If that makes sense.

ARIANA

Well it's not like we have anything else to go on.

FRANK

I have something else to show you.

FRANK sets up the last scene of *Forsaken* to play on the tele-vision.

ARIANA

Do we have to?

FRANK

Patience. This is serious. Watch my face as I view this scene.

FRANK plays the movie. His face, neck, and left arm twitch as before. But this time it is worse, causing him noticeable pain.

ARIANA

Huh?

FRANK

Did you see that?

ARIANA

You mean it happened automatically?

FRANK

Yes, worse than last time.

ARIANA

No way.

FRANK

Here, do it again, in slow motion this time, so you will know for sure.
(handing ARIANA the remote)

ARIANA plays the video in slow-motion as FRANK's body twitches identically as before in precise time with the film, only this time more slowly and painfully. There should be a weird intimacy to the way this is shown, like ARIANA is seeing something revealed at once from inside the film and inside Frank. Afterwards, FRANK experiences a moment of faintness or half-swooning and has to sit down.

FRANK

Don't worry. I'm OK.

ARIANA

Are you sure?

FRANK

Yes. I guess it is just affecting me more now.

ARIANA

To film fate with one's face. So how do you explain that?

FRANK

I don't.

INT. RICHARD AND SAMANTHA OVERBY'S HOUSE, BEDROOM – EVENING

RICHARD and SAMANTHA lie awake in bed after making

love. Their dialogue is interspersed with flashbacks of RICH-
ARD and CLAUDIA together, including having sex in
RICHARD's car after dropping FRANK at his hotel on the
night of MAX SLEIMAN's party.

SAMANTHA
Who was that woman with Frank at Max's party?

RICHARD
Which woman?

SAMANTHA
The one hanging out with you guys, with the crucifix
necklace? You seemed to know each other.

RICHARD
Oh that was Emina. She works with the European research group Oculus is partnering with.

SAMANTHA
Didn't she look a hell of a lot like your old friend Talia,
the waitress? Only a lot younger than she would look
now of course.

RICHARD
I thought the same. There's a striking resemblance. Café
O . . . What was the name of that place?

SAMANTHA
How can you forget? If Talia hadn't introduced us . . .

RICHARD
It'll come back.

SAMANTHA
You seem so distant after the party. Was it meeting

Frank?

RICHARD
It was great to meet Frank. He's a very interesting man.
Emina really took to him, kept talking about him when I
showed her around the lab.

SAMANTHA
You didn't tell me.

RICHARD
What's to tell?

SAMANTHA
Obviously we are on different channels. I worry that . . .

RICHARD
What?

SAMANTHA
Nothing.

RICHARD
I give you everything.

SAMANTHA
Not yourself, not you.

RICHARD
I don't know what to say to that.

SAMANTHA
See?

RICHARD
See what?

                    SAMANTHA
Either life is a lie or I am insane.

                    RICHARD
Please, honey, where is this coming from? Try to relax
and get some sleep.

                    SAMANTHA
Origin, Café Origin, that's the name of the place, where
it all never stops not beginning.

INT. MOUNTAIN LODGE, NEW HAMPSHIRE – EARLY
MORNING

GARY wakes, startled. TWO MEN and CLAUDIA enter
GARY'S holding room. As the TWO MEN restrain him,
CLAUDIA injects a drug into GARY's left arm with a syringe.
CLAUDIA observes him closely as the drug begins to take
effect. As the world fades around him, we see as if through
GARY's eyes while they remain looking at the gold cross
hanging from CLAUDIA's neck. Eventually everything goes
dark, and we see only the cross, flashing dimly in the void.
CLAUDIA then opens each of GARY's eyes, peering deep
into them with a small light.

                    CLAUDIA
OK, he is out. Bring him to the room in one hour.

INT. FRANK MASTRO'S APARTMENT ROOFTOP –
NIGHT

FRANK and ARIANA look out over the city.

                    ARIANA
I am afraid to go home. If someone took Gary,
maybe . . .

87

FRANK
Yes, it may be wise to escape New York.

FRANK
You can sleep in my study tonight.

ARIANA
Perfect. I'll feel right at home.

FRANK goes to set up the bed and ARIANA follows.

FRANK
It's funny, when you are young, the dream is to overturn everything. And then a new point arrives, imperceptibly passed, when the dream has overturned *you*.

ARIANA
At least some dreams are more real than this one.

FRANK
That is true.

ARIANA
Sweet dreams!
    (kissing FRANK on the cheek).

FRANK
Good night.

FRANK leaves the room. ARIANA looks around, finds the stack of tear photographs and browses through them, finding a police photograph of ASTRA's accident in which the blood on the street is circled where it forms a cross-like pattern. She then moves over ASTRA's photograph, drawn to it. A tear rolls down her cheek.

ARIANA
(whispering)
O darling, sweetheart, I love you. God protect you.

INT. MOUNTAIN LODGE, NEW HAMPSHIRE – EARLY
MORNING, BEFORE DAWN

MARSILIO stands outside as the TWO MEN help the CAN-
DIDATES into a small bus. Some appear dazed, others
wounded, one or two appear dead. All are unresponsive as
they are escorted onto the bus. The TWO MEN stand before
MARSILIO.

MARSILIO
Make sure each gets home safely. The ones who didn't
make it, treat the bodies very gently. It is dangerous to
anger them in this phase. After 72 hours, dispose as before, bringing me the thigh bones for charring.

TWO MEN
Yes, sir.

The TWO MEN drive off in the van and MARSILIO returns
inside to a basement room where CLAUDIA awaits. Inside
GARY is naked and restrained on the torture chair with head
immobilized and palms upward. An Oculus-type mask covers
his eyes and ears. There are various sensors on his body and
cameras are set up in the room to record the session. CLAU-
DIA walks over to GARY.

CLAUDIA
Gary, you are with us now. The room is safe. We are not
going to harm you. You will feel pain, but we are not
going to damage you. Do you understand?

GARY

OK, whatever. I hope you know what you are doing.

CLAUDIA

Think nothing. In three minutes the experience will be over.

CLAUDIA steps back, shuts off the lights, and readies a computer control pad which operates and is attached via wires to the torture chair. Dim illumination is provided by computer screens.

MARSILIO

Initiate.

CLAUDIA manipulates the control pad screen causing small robotic arms next to GARY's hands to move. The arms have slim nail-like blades which are positioned to pierce his palms. Another arm near his neck has a large needle which moves into position on the right side base of his skull. The nails and needle slow begin to enter GARY's body. MARSILIO closes his eyes as if trying to sense something. CLAUDIA carefully manipulates the controls and observes the scans and readings. MARSILIO appears to sense something and he motions to CLAUDIA to turn off the lights and screens so that it is pitch black in the room. Little by little faint colors in different tones begin to appear around the room with no visible source. The direction of the projection as it illuminates the faces and objects in the room shows that it is coming from the area of GARY's body. The colors slowly take on natural shapes consistent with a dream GARY might be having based on his recent experiences. As the forms become brighter and more defined, we see childhood scenes seen from a POV perspective, followed by representations of a more liquid, amniotic state. The projection crystallizes and brightens into a top-down shot of the scene of ASTRA's death, zooming towards her crushed head. When it reaches her head, there is a kind of boom and flash of light which whites out the room and blinds MARSIL-IO and CLAUDIA, who slump to the ground stunned. GARY yells out and suddenly the computer screens which CLAUDIA turned off turn on by themselves as if being hacked by an outside agent. Then the small robotic arm next to his right hand begins to withdraw the nail. GARY looks down in wonder and horror as the arm is then manipulated by an external force to undo the binding on his right hand. His reactions indicate that he is not using telekinesis or any kind of supernatural power. As soon as his right hand is free he reaches back and carefully withdraws the needle from his head. He then uses his right hand to free his left hand from the nail. With his left hand he is able to undo the brace holding his head in place. GARY frees his legs and runs out of the lodge into the countryside at dawn. Passing and startling some deer in an open field, he makes to a roadway where he halts in the highbeams of an oncoming car.

INT. CONVENT IN BROOKLYN – MORNING

SISTER CONNELLY sits in her room, reading softly out loud from the *Gospel of Thomas*.

> SISTER CONNELLY
> "When you make the two into one, and when you make the inner like the outer, and the outer like the inner, and the upper like the lower, and when you make male and female into a single one . . ."

INT. MOUNTAIN LODGE, NEW HAMPSHIRE – MORN-ING

MARSILIO and CLAUDIA return to consciousness after being stunned. MARSILIO is quiet and serious. CLAUDIA is disoriented and trembling as if not knowing where she is. MARSILIO tries to calm her down.

MARSILIO

Claudia!

CLAUDIA

Don't touch me! What the hell happened? What time is it?

MARSILIO

We are OK. Calm down.

CLAUDIA

Where is Gary?

MARSILIO

He escaped.

CLAUDIA

How . . . ?

MARSILIO plays back the camera recordings.

MARSILIO

Check the data.

CLAUDIA reviews information on the computer.

CLAUDIA

The scan record is intact. We have full data from the trial. But someone hacked the controls.

MARSILIO

I see that.

CLAUDIA

There is a signature on the command log.

                    MARSILIO
Let me see.

MARSILIO walks over to the computer.

                    CLAUDIA
Super non contra. OSL.

                    MARSILIO
Above not against.

                    CLAUDIA
The spider?

                    MARSILIO
Yes. No. Don't ask. Take everything offline and get me
Richard right away. He needs to fly out and collect
these results in person immediately.

                    CLAUDIA
What does this mean?

                    MARSILIO
That this data will no doubt provide the correct sequencing of the impressions from the 1978 dispensa-
tion. We have found it, but are not the only ones.

                    CLAUDIA
Who is?

                    MARSILIO
Precisely.

INT. DINER IN NEW HAMPSHIRE – MORNING

GARY, dressed in donated clothes and with band aids on each

of his hands, is eating a hearty breakfast at a busy diner counter. A gentle old man sitting next to him pats him on the back in reassurance and GARY smiles in response, comforted.

> SISTER CONNELLY (V.O.) (cont'd)
> ". . . so that the male will not be male nor the female be female, when you make eyes in place of an eye, a hand in place of a hand, a foot in place of a foot, an image in place of an image, then you will enter the kingdom."

EXT. YOGA STUDIO IN MALIBU – MIDDAY

SAMANTHA and CAROL SLEIMAN are taking a yoga class on a lovely terrace overlook the Pacific Ocean.

> YOGA INSTRUCTOR
> . . . be grateful for the opportunity to bless yourself with this practice. Now, as you move into your day, connect yourself with all that you feel. There is no separation. Hear the ocean. You are the ocean. You are depth, passion, abundance. Smell the sweet air. You are the air. You are gentleness, peace, generosity. Feel the sunlight. You are the sun. You are wisdom, vision, truth. And above all, you are love.

As the class concludes, SAMANTHA and CAROL walk out together.

> CAROL
> Wasn't that wonderful?

SAMANTHA doesn't answer.

> CAROL
> Are you not feeling well?

SAMANTHA
No, I'm OK. I'm just not myself these days.

CAROL
What is it?

SAMANTHA
Do you remember . . . ?

CAROL
What?

SAMANTHA
Nevermind.

EXT. FRANK AND ARIANA DRIVING IN UPSTATE NEW
YORK – MORNING

ARIANA
Where are we going?

FRANK
An old friend of mine, Sol, has, or had, a place in the
Adirondacks, off the grid. I have the keys.

ARIANA
Sol, isn't that . . .

FRANK
Yes, the cameraman.

ARIANA
Whatever happened to him?

FRANK
He disappeared several years ago. Left his family a

cryptic letter that he was leaving for good. The family asked me to check up on the place.

                    ARIANA
Find anything?

                    FRANK
No, only a few signs that he had been there. They assume he died somewhere in the mountains, that the blindness caught up with him.

                    ARIANA
Suicide? So strange. I just had the weirdest déjà vu, like being in a film I've already seen but can't remember.

                    FRANK
It's a universal feeling.

                    ARIANA
Abandon all hope, ye who exit.

                    FRANK
A non sequitur?

                    ARIANA
No. I was thinking that everything must have an exit.

                    FRANK
I don't see one.

                    ARIANA
Nor I.

ARIANA's phone rings and she answers.

                    ARIANA
Hello?

                    GARY (V.O.)
Ariana!

                    ARIANA
Gary! Where are you? Are you OK?

                    GARY (V.O.)
Yes, don't worry. Somebody took me, but I escaped.

                    ARIANA
O my God.
    (to FRANK)
It's Gary, he's alright!

                    GARY (V.O.)
I am taking a bus to the city.

                    ARIANA
No, it's not safe. We are driving upstate.

FRANK motions to have the phone.

                    FRANK
Gary, this is Frank.

                    GARY (V.O.)
Frank?

                    FRANK
We talked to Sister Connelly yesterday. Take a bus to
Albany. Can you do that?

> GARY (V.O.)
> OK. Albany.

> FRANK
> We will pick you up at the corner of Lodge St. and Maiden Lane. To be safe. There's an old white building there. Got it?

> GARY
> Yes, Lodge St and Maiden Lane. Old white building.

ARIANA takes the phone back.

> ARIANA
> Gary.

> GARY (V.O.)
> I will be there! You are not going to believe what happened.

> ARIANA
> I don't. I love you!

> GARY (V.O.)
> I love you.

GARY hangs up the phone.

> ARIANA
> I am so happy.

> FRANK
> A tunnel at the beginning of the light!

INT. A PASSENGER BUS – AFTERNOON

A shot of the passengers in transit on the bus, with GARY among them. The shot should accentuate the heads of the people, which are hooked up to various devices and/or watching drop down movie screens. Though tuned into different experiences, the majority of the heads rock and bob in unconscious unison to the movement of the bus, communicating a dark sense of their submersion in the world, like Plato's Allegory of the Cave.

INT. PRIVATE JET – DAY

RICHARD OVERBY picks up the phone.

> RICHARD
>
> Max.

> MAX (V.O.)
>
> Yes.

> RICHARD
>
> Does the name Gary Thatcher mean anything?

> MAX (V.O.)
>
> No, I can't say it does.

> RICHARD
>
> He's the graduate student Frank was joking about at the party. Seems he's something more than your average fan boy. The Italians inform me that he has some *sensitive* information.

> MAX (V.O.)
>
> That is unfortunate.

> RICHARD
>
> Maybe not. But we need to speak with him as soon as

possible. I'm flying out East now.

                    MAX (V.O.)
I understand. Will let you know if I hear anything.

                    RICHARD
Very good.

EXT. MASONIC TEMPLE, ALBANY – EARLY EVENING

FRANK and ARIANA wait in front of the entrance for GARY, before the twin columns capped by stone spheres, similar to the columns in front of the White Castle in SISTER CON-NELLY's vision.[60]

                    ARIANA
Have you been here before?

                    FRANK
When I was little boy. My grandfather Mario, we called him Mo, worked up here as a stonemason and liked to show me the buildings.

A BOY, lagging behind his family, walks before FRANK and ARIANA, carelessly bouncing a blue ball.

                    ARIANA
Play marbles with memory.

ARIANA sees GARY approaching and they run to greet each other, embracing.

                    FRANK
What to say? Let's get going.

ARIANA

Everything!

They enter the car nearby.

ARIANA

What happened to your hands?

GARY

Nothing too serious. A sweet old man in North Conway bandaged them.

FRANK

We will be safe at Sol's.

ARIANA

You must tell Gary about the dream, and the nerve thing, and what Sister Connelly said.

GARY

I never meant for anyone to see the video. Didn't know what I was doing. Forgive me.

ARIANA

No one except everyone on the internet! Forgiven.

GARY

Yes, there may be a small contradiction there.

FRANK

Everything is contradiction. Gary, I am sorry to have brushed you off last week. Tell us all.

GARY

I was sitting at home Friday night when two men came to the door . . .

INT. RICHARD and SAMANTHA OVERBY'S HOUSE –
MIDDAY

SAMANTHA is looking through an album of photographs
from her and RICHARD's wedding. She is trying to find a
photograph of TALIA/CLAUDIA. She finds only a group picture where CLAUDIA'S face is eclipsed by someone else's
head. Around the head is a subtle shadow, suggestive of a dark
nimbus or halo. ROBERT screeches his car into the driveway
and enters the living room.

                    SAMANTHA
        Robert?

                    ROBERT
        Is Richard here?

                    SAMANTHA
        He had to fly back east. Didn't he tell you?

                    ROBERT
        Fuck!

                    SAMANTHA
        What's the matter?

                    ROBERT
        Nothing. I just need . . .

ROBERT goes into RICHARD's study. He searches the desk
and bookshelves and eventually finds a small box which he
forces open with a letter opener inside of which are two old
keys. He takes the keys as SAMANTHA enters the room.

                    SAMANTHA
        What are you looking for?

ROBERT
Nothing. I thought . . .

ROBERT, who previously appeared quite agitated, now walks out of the room very slowly in a non-responsive, automatic way.

SAMANTHA
Where are you going?

ROBERT walks out to the car. SAMANTHA follows.

SAMANTHA
Robert, what are you doing?

ROBERT
I am . . .

ROBERT gets in his car and drives off. SAMANTHA gets in her car and follows.

EXT/INT. WOODS IN UPSTATE NEW YORK – SUNSET

FRANK et al. drive through a dark wood-lined road then turn uphill onto Sol Francken's eroded driveway. They pull up to his house, which is run-down in a classic Appalachian way (debris in the yard, overgrown bushes, unkempt exterior). All exit the car, walk up to the porch, and FRANK opens the door.

FRANK
There is no power here, just an old generator out back that might prefer not to work.

ARIANA and GARY check out the place as FRANK goes out back. The cabin is clean but old and dusty from lack of use. The evening sun streams in the windows, illuminating the golden motes of dust.

> GARY
> That thou seest, man, become too thou must; / God, if thou seest God, dust, if thou seest dust.

> ARIANA
> I see you!

ARIANA joyfully embraces GARY so that they fall back together onto a single bed, causing more dust to be stirred into the air.

EXT. OLD CEMETARY IN LOS ANGELES – EVENING

SAMANTHA's car follows ROBERT's into a cemetery. ROBERT parks and walks to the pyramidal mausoleum where he was previously with CLAUDIA and RICHARD. SAMANTHA observes from a distance. ROBERT opens the door with one of the keys and enters. SAMANTHA sits in the car for a while, pondering what to do, then gets out and starts walking slowly toward the mausoleum.

INT. SOL'S CABIN IN UPSTATE NEW YORK – LATE AT NIGHT

FRANK, ARIANA, and GARY are sitting drinking bourbon around a coffee table lit by one small lamp.

> GARY
> Clearly we are beyond the threshold of coincidence here. The copy of the *Spiritual Exercises* I saw in Rome was torn like in Frank's dream.

> FRANK
> The Green Man must have it.

ARIANA

For real? This is too much. Like a movie about a conspiracy about a movie. A cosmic secret leaked by occult
forces out of the Pope's corpse into the imaginal fabric
of *Forsaken*, affecting whomsoever it touches, the
Templar key to headless seeing, coveted by the Illuminati to maintain cinematic control of the world?[61] Seri-
ously? I think we all need to get some sleep.

GARY

It is late.

FRANK

I will turn off the generator to save fuel. Here are some
candles.

FRANK exits and GARY and ARIANA light the candles. The
lamp goes out as the power is cut.

ARIANA
(closing her eyes)
You can try to explain the video tomorrow.

GARY
Zero, four, three, three.

ARIANA

Tomorrow!

ARIANA gets up and walks down a dark hallway and then up
some steep steps towards the bathroom carrying a candle.

ARIANA
Man it's dark here.

ARIANA enters the bathroom and places her candle and

matches on the sink. While looking in the mirror the candle
tips over and goes out. She fumbles around in the dark.

                    ARIANA
        Hey can somebody bring me a light!

Receiving no answer she begins fumbling around for the candle which has rolled away. She then starts feeling her way
back along the walls towards the top of the stairwell.

                    ARIANA
        So this is what it was like, to be Sol.

As ARIANA says this the lightbulb in a wall lamp at the top of
stairwell faintly glows, providing just enough illumination for
ARIANA to catch herself before stepping off the landing.

                    ARIANA
        Weird.

GARY arrives carrying his candle at the bottom of the steps.
The lamp dims out.

                    GARY
        Everything OK?

                    ARIANA
        Yes, my light went out. I called for you.

                    GARY
        I was outside helping Frank with the generator.

                    ARIANA
        O that must have been it.

GARY comes up the stairs and all retire for the night.

EXT. OLD CEMETARY IN LOS ANGELES – EVENING

ROBERT walks down the dark spiral stairs of the mausoleum to the lower chamber. He opens the door with one of the keys. As he enters it a motion sensor triggers a red LED light which illuminates the room. In the back of the room are air shafts with grates on them. There is a faint sound of running water. In the back center of the room, between the air shafts, is an ornate casket-like box, black and gold, set at a sloping angle with the head higher than the feet. A pipe leads from the upper part of the wall into the top of the casket at one side. On the other side, there is a large covered basin with a pipe leading into the casket. The front of the casket has a double door-like lid and an ornate grated opening. At the foot of the casket another pipe descends into the floor. At the side of the room is a shelf with several towels, bottles of water, a variety of substances in glass and crystal bottles, and some instruments of torture and pleasure. At the head of the casket is a strange geometric kind of keyhole. ROBERT examines the keyhole, which is obviously too large for either of the keys he took from RICHARD's study. He tries to open the casket with his hands to no avail. He grabs one of the implements and inserts it into the hole, trying to force the lock. He partially succeeds, loosening the other, which he is then able to pry open.

INT. SOL'S CABIN IN UPSTATE NEW YORK – MIDNIGHT

ARIANA opens her eyes in bed, woken by a strange buzzing/humming sound. She gets up and looks around, unable to tell exactly where it is coming from, but it is louder in the living room, where she notices that the outdated television is faintly glowing. She flips a light switch and tries to turn on a lamp, but nothing happens, showing that the electricity is not on. She goes to the television and sits before the screen listening to the sound. She touches the screen with her right finger and as she does so light gathers and glows around it in a specific color. Simultaneously, the sound she is hearing in the room changes tone. As she focuses on the tone, another area of subtle light, different in color, appears on the screen and she brings her left hand to touch its center. Another tone is added to the sounds she hears pervading the room. The areas of light begin slowly to move, and she follows them with her fingers. The movements increase in speed and assume the form of a complex pattern matched with sounds. She continues to move her hands in synchronicity with the lights on the screen, paradoxically as if remembering the pattern more and more the more complicated and fast it becomes, like a weird combination of a Ouija board and the electronic Simon Says memory game. The pattern of lights has an overall cross-like and four-square structure and the sounds repeat in a 0-4-3-3 pattern. ARIANA starts sounding out the tones with her own voice, entering a trance more and more intense, so that she appears to be both musician and instrument of the pattern, both played by and playing the forms being communicated through the screen. The volume becomes loud enough to wake FRANK who comes into the room. What he sees shocks and terrifies him: ARIANA's body kneeling down in front of the radiant screen, her torso detached from her limbs floating in the air, her arms still moving in unison with the pattern of light and color, and her severed head floating in the center of the room, vibrating with sound.

FRANK

Ariana!

As FRANK screams her name he drops to the floor unconscious and the screen goes white.

EXT. OLD CEMETARY IN LOS ANGELES – EVENING

ROBERT slowly pries open the two doors of the casket to reveal the SIBYL, an emaciated middle-aged woman whose four limbs have been amputated. Her stumps are fitted with gold coverings which are attached to the interior of the casket. The SIBYL is naked except for a kind of harness, connected to the waste tubes, which covers her genitals like a chastity belt. She appears tranquil and breathing softly, as if sleeping, eyes closed. The interior of the casket is fitted with a patterned concentric array of different colored gemstones in a general cross pattern. The SIBYL has golden hair, except for a spot on the top of her head which is bald and fitted with an ornament framing an opening into the crown. This is evidently where the crystal key previously carried by CLAUDIA is to be inserted. Entranced in a kind of reverie, ROBERT begins to slowly probe the crown opening of the SIBYL with his right hand while touching other parts of her body with his left. The SIBYL stirs gently, slowly opening her eyes which are a striking sea-green color. Robert stares fixedly into her eyes. The SIBYL begins to open her mouth and make subtle sounds as if beginning to whisper something. ROBERT leans closer. Suddenly the SIBYL, as if startled and realizing her violation in a shock, becomes agitated and begins to shiver and writhe. ROBERT, still entranced, places his ear to her mouth. With a screech the SIBYL bites down hard on ROBERT's ear. Stunned and bleeding, ROBERT screams and fumbles for a towel to cover his wound. Then SAMANTHA enters the room.

SAMANTHA
My God Robert what the hell? You're hurt!

ROBERT
Fuck!! You should not be here.

SAMANTHA
Robert what's matter? What is this place?

SAMANTHA now sees the SIBYL and begins screaming is shock and horror. ROBERT gags her with the towel he was using to stanch his ear wound.

> ROBERT
> You cannot be here!

He takes a cord from the shelf and binds SAMANTHA's wrists to something near the base of the casket. He tapes the gag in place over her mouth and stares as SAMANTHA crumples to the floor in confused terror.

> ROBERT
> OK, we will deal with this.

ROBERT takes out his cell phone and makes a call.

> ROBERT
> Richard, this is Robert. I have a serious problem here.

EXT. SOL'S CABIN IN UPSTATE NEW YORK – LATE MORNING

ARIANA and GARY are sitting having coffee on the porch.

> GARY
> Do you think I should tell Frank about my dream, of being Astra?

> ARIANA
> I don't think so. Not now. Too much as is.

> GARY
> Right.

ARIANA

And I had the strangest dream last night. I was communicating to Sol through the television in a secret language of light and sound.

GARY

How'd you know it was Sol?

ARIANA

I don't know. It just was. Like how a voice just *is* someone. And even though I was dreaming it, it was also like the dream was dreaming me, playing me, but dreaming me actually being there for real.

GARY

A lucid dream?

ARIANA

Maybe, I don't know.

FRANK walks out from the house.

FRANK

It wasn't a dream.

GARY

Morning Frank. Find Sol's secret stash last night? We found you passed out in the living room and moved you to the couch.

FRANK

It wasn't a dream Ariana. This might be one. But what I saw last night was *real*.

ARIANA

What are you talking about?

FRANK

You, in front of the television. Your head was . . . separated from your body.

ARIANA

What??

GARY

You are saying that you saw Ariana's dream?

FRANK

No I am saying she wasn't dreaming.

ARIANA

So what was I doing?

FRANK

You were moving your hands on the screen in a pattern of lights and sounds, and . . . floating in the room, in parts.

ARIANA

Floating? Sol was telling me something so familiar, but I can't remember it now.

GARY

And her body appeared severed, limb from limb?

FRANK

Yes!

ARIANA

Like the saints Sister C mentioned. What are those numbers you said last night?

GARY

Zero, Four, Three, Three.

ARIANA

That's the pattern Sol was using. So I was sleepwalking?

FRANK

The video?

GARY

Yes, the numbers are just a placeholder, for something you can't get your head around. One must *do* it, like you did in *Forsaken*.

FRANK

I didn't fucking do that!

ARIANA

Exactly. Like me. Without knowing it. So, love, how did you . . . *not* figure it out?

GARY

Chinnamasta, that's a three-plus-one form: three bodies in four parts with three streams of blood. That is a symbol for headless seeing as a fourth dimension. I look at the cross and write three threes on the lower points and one on the top. Three threes plus one one. The sum is ten, one plus zero, one. A total form. Then Sister Connelly reminds me about the five wounds, how the head wounds do not count, so those wounds are "beheaded."[62] Now the Indian goddess always holds her head in her left hand, like the witch in *Forsaken*. So on the cross diagram, you decapitate the one, making it a zero and adding one to the left 3. Zero, four, three, three. I saw myself as that and . . .

FRANK

And what?

GARY

I don't know!

ARIANA

A self-beheading medieval witch in a 70s horror flick showed you how to see beyond perspective and project imagination into matter.

GARY

Real special effects. Cinematic vision. Seeing from *outside* your head. This world is a screen.

ARIANA

Cut and paste.

FRANK

OK, no more coincidences. This is so scary and beautiful and real I can barely think. Clearly we've been touched, or spliced, by something . . .

ARIANA

Sacred.

FRANK

Right. Or we are totally fucked, screwed in the head.

GARY

Forsaken is a miracle.

ARIANA

Yeah, but of what?

FRANK
If Sol could tell us what he saw, what blinded him . . .

ARIANA
That's it! He must still be here.

GARY
Or what's left of him.

INT. MOUNTAIN LODGE, NEW HAMPSHIRE – LATE MORNING

RICHARD arrives and walks towards the bar of the lodge where CLAUDIA BRANDINI is seated alone, smoking.

CLAUDIA
Sorted out?

RICHARD
Yes. Marsilio will take Samantha to the clinic for safe-keeping.

CLAUDIA
Life is full of surprises. Will Gary Thatcher work for Oculus?

RICHARD
It may not be very difficult to persuade him. Tell me about the new data.

CLAUDIA
The patterns from Gary's trial match perfectly, to the thirty-ninth prime, the impressions retrieved in '78.

RICHARD
Retrieved?

CLAUDIA
Ah, now you can hear the story.

BEGIN FLASHBACK: INT. PAPAL APARTMENTS, HALLWAY – EARLY MORNING, 1978

A CARDINAL leads MARSILIO BARBI and TWO MEN down the hallway. BARBI's appearance is the same as in earlier scenes, only barely younger, as if he ages at a supernaturally slow rate.

CARDINAL
Do not worry, Signor Barbi, I am certain that His Holiness will be delighted to see you this morning. He rises early.

MARSILIO
I would not want to disturb him.

As they walk down the hall, the TWO MEN, without being noticed, ready pistols. All arrive before the door to the POPE's chambers, which the CARDINAL opens.

CARDINAL
Please.

The CARDINAL walks away. MARSILIO and the TWO MEN enter and discover the body of the POPE, killed as in the opening scene. The POPE'S head is stuck on a spear which is upright and placed in the body's left hand, as if he is holding it. The face of the POPE's head appears to be softly smiling. BARBI and the TWO MEN are taken aback with horror and shock.

MARSILIO
Giuda ballerino![63] But how in God's name? Who could

get here before us? On the very day. *Who???!!!*

MARSILIO looks around, examines the body. He finds the wound in the POPE's side and places his finger inside.

MARSILIO

I do not believe this. It is impossible.

MARSILIO feels the parchment within the body and begins to slowly pull it out, showing part of the Prime Number Cross design. As he does so, one of the TWO MEN reaches out to touch the POPE's severed head, which has lines of black caked ashes descending from the eyes and nose and mouth.

MAN

Cristo santo.

MARSILIO

Non toccare!!!

The MAN pulls back.

MAN

We must call the alarm immediately, or they will suspect us.

MARSILIO

Quick. Scrape the black dust from the head into that envelope there.

The TWO MEN gather the ashes as MARSILIO folds the parchment and places it in his green suit. Once finished, they all begin shouting for help.

END FLASHBACK.

                    RICHARD
        Fuck.

                    CLAUDIA
        (after a long pause)
        That's what I was thinking.

INT. SOL'S HOUSE – LATE MORNING

ARIANA and GARY are searching around the back of SOL's cabin, walking towards the generator shed.

                    GARY
        . . . seven rings of twenty-four integers, one through one-sixty-eight, like a huge clock or medieval cosmos.

                    ARIANA
        Now we have to get tattoos.

                    GARY
        Prime number cross?

                    ARIANA
        With the twins colored in black.

                    GARY
        Why black?

                    ARIANA
        Because the twin primes are the sacred pupils of headless seeing. Joined by separation, separated by joining.

                    GARY
        And they sum to ten or one plus zero for one vision.

They enter the shed, which is dark and dusty.

ARIANA
And if vision were to see itself?

GARY
"Thou canst not see my face; for Man shall not see me,
and live."

ARIANA
Look! There is a small door here. Like to a root cellar.

GARY
That makes sense. They didn't have generators when
this place was built.

ARIANA
Of course! All roads lead to Rome. Gimme the flash-
light and go get Frank.

GARY
Be careful.

ARIANA
(winking)
Not to worry, I'm a woman.

GARY goes out to get FRANK, who is sitting down gazing at
an unopened handwritten letter.

GARY
Frank!

FRANK looks up and stares at GARY in silence with an intensely moved look, as if recognizing GARY in a new way.

GARY
Frank come with me. We found something.

FRANK folds the letter into his pocket and follows GARY in silence. As they return towards the shed ARIANA screams. They rush in to find ARIANA in the cellar shining the flash-light on the remains of SOL's body, who appears to have died from spontaneous combustion. Parts of his extremities remain, arms and legs, but the rest is black and silver ashes, which swirl in the air.

FRANK
O my God.

They stare in silent wonder at the eerie scene.

ARIANA
Probably best if no one finds him.

GARY
Precisely.

INT. MOUNTAIN LODGE, NEW HAMPSHIRE – MIDDAY
CLAUDIA and RICHARD go to the basement room where GARY was tortured. CLAUDIA leans over the chair and RICHARD binds her wrists to it, then undresses himself and her.

CLAUDIA
The mask.

RICHARD places the Oculus mask over her eyes and presses a button to initiate a sequencing of impressions. Her gold crucifix dangles in the air.

CLAUDIA
Whip me.

RICHARD flogs CLAUDIA to excitement.

CLAUDIA

Fuck me.

RICHARD places a black hood over his head and penetrates CLAUDIA from behind as she stares directly into the projector.

CLAUDIA

No, here.

CLAUDIA reaches back to redirect RICHARD's penis, so that its place of entry remains ambivalent. RICHARD penetrates her with increasing intensity. CLAUDIA begins to have a very strong orgasm, her abdominal muscles contracting through long and deep but not very vocal breaths. Her brow furrows intensely to suggest a connection to the third eye.

CLAUDIA

O God, O God! It is there, right there in front of me.

RICHARD

Tell me. Tell me what you see.

CLAUDIA climaxes as the energy of her body dies down with aftershocks of the orgasm. RICHARD ejaculates holding her neck and bringing his mouth to her ear.

RICHARD

Tell me!

CLAUDIA

Nothing. I see nothing.

INT. ROOT CELLAR OUTSIDE SOL'S HOUSE – MIDDAY

Slowly and silently, ARIANA, GARY, and FRANK collect the

remains of SOL's body, inevitably inhaling and getting covered in the ashes, which they carry away in a small container after burying the limbs in the ground.

INT. MAUSOLEUM – MIDDAY

We see darkness and then a light as someone opens the door to the mausoleum chamber where SAMANTHA is bound and gagged. TWO MEN enter the room, place a black hood over her head, inject her with a sedative, and carry her away. As the door closes behind them, the camera remains for a while in the room, slowly zooming towards the SIBYL's casket.

EXT. FREEWAY IN NEW YORK CITY – EARLY EVENING

FRANK, GARY, and ARIANA are driving back to the city.

> ARIANA
> What will you do with Sol's ashes?

> FRANK
> I don't know.

They look out over Calvary Cemetery in Queens from the BQE, with the skyline of Manhattan in the background.

> FRANK
> I think it's time for me to leave this city.

> GARY
> Where?

> FRANK
> I don't know.

The car pulls up to a block in Brooklyn

                    FRANK
          Will you two be OK?

                    GARY
          Sure.

                    ARIANA
          I'm not worried anymore.

                    FRANK
          Good, here we are.

The car pulls up outside Gary and Ariana's apartment. GARY and ARIANA say goodbye, start to walk away, and then pause.

                    GARY
          Hey Frank, what were you reading, before we found Sol?

                    FRANK
          A letter from an old friend.

                    ARIANA
          Who?

                    FRANK
          Rebecca, Rebecca Toma.

                    GARY
          What did it say?

                    FRANK
          I haven't read it.

ARIANA
(winking)
Secret.

EXT/INT. OCULUS MEDIA LABORATORIES, CALIFOR-
NIA – MORNING

MARSILIO and RICHARD walk in the grounds outside the
Oculus laboratories. The O.M. logo is visible in the background.

RICHARD
Is there any reason for O.M. to be concerned any further
with this *Forsaken* business?

MARSILIO
I don't believe so. Mastro's movements will be moni-
tored.

RICHARD
Good. And Thatcher?

MARSILIO
Give him time. He will come around. Meanwhile, we
have what we need.

CLAUDIA exits the building and joins them.

CLAUDIA
Gentlemen, the computations are finished. Please come
inside. The results will please you.

All walk inside the laboratory and enter a room with a large
screen. CLAUDIA brings up a series of diagrams and numbers
on the screen, including one resembling the Prime Number
Cross.

CLAUDIA
As you can see, by delivering all permutations simultaneously at maximum intensity via the filter modelled on
the Thatcher data, we have achieved fully differentiated
personalization with 97% awareness in both subjects.

MARSILIO
Fantastic.

RICHARD
Just as we thought. Now, by sequencing the intersection
of the twins' divergent impressional expenditures, we
can move forward immediately with synthesizing a matrix whose effects will be temporary to within 3% un-
predictability.

MARSILIO
The global partners will be happy with anything under
4%.

RICHARD
And Gemma and Emma, how are they holding up?

CLAUDIA
As anticipated, the frequency of sharp waves in the hip-
pocampus is extreme. The experiment has left them in-
capable of forgetting.

RICHARD walks over to adjacent one-way observation windows, followed by CLAUDIA and MARSILIO. The windows
look into separate rooms containing GEMMA and EMMA.
The rooms are furnished normally, like dorm rooms, containing a few personal effects. Where GEMMA appears abnormal-
ly excited, as if in a mad state of constant reaction to a pletho-
ra of hallucinations or subjective mental movies, EMMA sits
calmly at her computer, writing emails, browsing the web, and

listening to music.

>   CLAUDIA
> Yet, as you can see, the behaviors could not be more
> different. Where GEMMA is effectively insane, EMMA
> is as normal as ever. Yet neurologically, they have never
> been more identical.

>   MARSILIO
> Amazing. How beautiful they are like this to me. So
> perfectly, differently *the same*.

>   RICHARD
> Themselves forever.

INT. MEDICAL CLINIC, CALIFORNIA – LATE MORN-
ING

SAMANTHA wakes up in an elegant room overlooking the
beach, golden light on her face. A NURSE enters the room.

>   NURSE
> Good morning Samantha.

>   SAMANTHA
> Where am I?

>   NURSE
> Do not worry. There was an accident. You are safe now.

>   SAMANTHA
> Accident?

>   NURSE
> The Doctor will explain everything. Try to rest.

SAMANTHA

Rest?

The NURSE exits the room. SAMANTHA stares at the sun as it sets behind the horizon of the ocean. She is confused. She looks down towards her body and kicks and throws off the covers to discover that her limbs have been amputated, at the knees and elbows. She stares at herself in shock and starts to weep. The room darkens as the sunlight fades away.

INT. TATTOO PARLOR, BROOKLYN – EVENING

GARY and ARIANA sit and smile at each other in adjacent chairs getting tattoos of the Prime Number Cross on their arms. The camera hovers above them to highlight the disembodiment of perspective.

INT. FRANK'S APARTMENT – NIGHT

FRANK sits in his study. To his right is the letter from RE-BECCA found at SOL's house, still unopened. The camera hovers around FRANK's head the way it did earlier. He begins reading the letter, whose words we cannot make out, except for the signature, "Rebecca Toma," including a small stamp based on the form of the Narcissus flower. He puts the letter down and holds his head in his hands as the camera looks down from above on him, sobbing. A tear falls on the Narcissus emblem, causing the ink to start to bleed. FRANK watches as the ink bleeds out in branch like forms. After it stops, he takes a photograph of it, which he blows up on the screen. Astonished, he sees that the ink has formed into the ROMA-AMOR square surrounding a face. FRANK pulls out a still from *Forsaken* showing Cinnaedea's severed head at the moment it turns young again and we see that the face closely resembles it. FRANK's face and neck twitch as they did before. He feels faint and swoons to the ground.

INT. MAX SLEIMMAN'S HOUSE – NIGHTIME

MAX and CAROL sit watching a late night television talk show in which ROBERT is being interviewed.

> HOST
> *Kingdom of Night*, wow. You must be pretty happy with how the movie performed this week.

> ROBERT
> Yes, the whole thing is a dream come true. Max Sleiman is an awesome director and human being. It has been an honor to work with him and his team.

CAROL places her hand on MAX's arm in a gesture of appreciation.

> HOST
> Your family must be very proud.

> ROBERT
> I owe my success to them, especially my step-father Richard and most of all my mother, who was so supportive from day one.
> (waving to the camera)
> Hi Mom!

> HOST
> So sweet. Now, tell us about your work with Oculus Media, the whole "neurocinema" thing that's got everyone speculating.

> ROBERT
> It's very exciting.

HOST

What is "neurocinema" exactly?

ROBERT

Well, all cinema is neurocinema of course, meaning that we see it with our brains. What Oculus is doing is taking the process to the next level, developing a way to harness the power of our imagination so that the film-viewing experience is much more individualized and interactive.

HOST

Like a video game?

ROBERT

To some degree, yes. But we're talking about a new level of intensity, not only audio-visual effects, but also affective and emotional qualities on par with what you might only experience in dreams, or real life. They call it AS for Acute Subjectivity.

HOST

As in as real as reality?

ROBERT

Exactly.

HOST

So how does it work, exactly?

ROBERT

The science is way over my head. But basically, O.M. has found a 100% natural, non-invasive, non-chemical way of activating the part of the brain responsible for *lucid dreaming*, in sync with algorithms embedded within the movie stream.

The HOST looks impressed, then hams it up by making a joke of looking at his hands to check if he is dreaming or not.

> HOST
> How many fingers do you see? Pinch me!

The audience laughs. ROBERT pinches him playfully.

> ROBERT
> But seriously, this is the real deal. And it's so authentic, a leap beyond those alienating VR systems.

> HOST
> You'll never catch me wearing one of those masks, bro. Maybe if I was ugly!

ROBERT looks uneasy for a moment and brings his hand to his ear where the SIBYL bit him.

> HOST
> Great to have you on the show, Robert. You look great! Ladies and gentlemen, Robert Mastro!

EXT. LEONARDO DA VINCI INTERNATIONAL AIRPORT, ROME – LATE MORNING

FRANK arrives and gets in a taxi, which takes him through sunny Rome, dropping him off at an elegant apartment building. An ASSISTANT is there to greet him as he gets out of the taxi. FRANK carries with him, in a small container, SOL's ashes.

> ASSISTANT
> Signor Mastro. Welcome to Roma. Please come this way.

INT. MEDICAL CLINIC, CALIFORNIA – MIDDLE OF THE NIGHT

A full moon shines over the ocean and into the room where SAMANTHA lies in bed. Suddenly she opens her eyes and with steady determination wiggles painfully out of her restraints and onto the floor supported by her still bandaged limbs. She crawls out the window, over a small garden wall and into the vegetation leading towards the beach. As she eventually makes it down to the surf, blood appears on her bandages, which eventually become loose and fall off as she enters the water. Barely able to stay afloat in the water, she resembles a sinuous and wounded water creature, a form losing its humanity in a desperate yet ecstatic dissolution in the ocean. The scene should look and feel primordial, like SAMANTHA is passing in death through the evolutionary mystery of birth.

INT. ELEGANT BUILDING, ROME – MIDDAY

The ASSISTANT leads FRANK through the building to a large room where REBECCA TOMA stands surrounded by a small group of people. There is various film equipment and crates around the room. REBECCA is elegant, beautiful, and about Frank's age, with the charismatic aura of an older starlet like Stefania Casini. The ASSISTANT silently points her out to FRANK, as we hear some late 70s giallo/horror synth playing in the background.[64] REBECCA sees FRANK and they move across the room to greet each other.

                    REBECCA
        Frank!

FRANK and REBECCA embrace warmly.

REBECCA

Everyone! I'd like you to meet Frank Mastro. Frank
will be directing the shoot next week. Please see to his
every need. This is an especially important one.

REBECCA and FRANK walk together to sit in a smaller room
with comfortable chairs, behind which is another room whose
door is slightly ajar. They sit, happy and moved to see each
other again.

FRANK

This schedule, this shoot – I was studying it the whole
flight over and it seems, frankly, impossible.

REBECCA

Don't worry. It will all work out. We need this one finished by the twenty ninth. It is the thirty-ninth anniver-
sary, and three plus three plus three plus three equals
three.

FRANK

OK. One question. May I ask who I am working for?

REBECCA

Yes, sweetheart, you may.

An assistant stands before FRANK to whom REBECCA gestures to hand over the container holding SOL's ashes, which
FRANK does. The assistant enters the room behind whose
door is ajar. REBECCA reaches over to close the door that is
ajar, showing us behind it a hint of one of the THREE FIG-
URES.

REBECCA

Only the best, Frank, only the best.

INT. GARY AND ARIANA'S APARTMENT – MORNING

GARY and ARIANA are hanging out. GARY sits in front of his television screen. An elegant ebony, paper-sized box with the O.M. logo rests on the coffee table in front of him.

> GARY
> O my God, Ariana! You must see this. You are not going to believe it. You cannot *not* see this.

ARIANA rushes over to see what GARY is seeing. Both stare at the screen in astonishment and wonder.

INT. CONVENT IN BROOKLYN – DAYTIME

A group of NUNS, in blue habits, are gathered in a common room listening to the news on the radio. Among them, off to the side, is SISTER CONNELLY.

> NEWSPERSON
> First in the news today, reports are increasing around the world of a strange and increasingly evident new kind of black anomaly or glitch affecting not only most forms of visual media but human vision itself. Dubbed "blind matter," "chaos ash," and more commonly, "black dust," the phenomenon has no scientifically known boundary or origin and is causing confusion, fascination, and concern worldwide. As myriad theories are advanced by individuals and institutions as to its cause, from some form of mass hallucination to a deep cosmological weather event, governments are urging people to remain calm as there is no evidence that the "black dust" has any effects other than its own appearance. Meanwhile, new evidence of "black dust" is piling up, leaving its mark on everything from children's cartoons to terrorist execution videos. Even more dis-

concerting is the fact that the unknown phenomenon is both objective and subjective in a spontaneous and inexplicable way, sometimes appearing to many persons at once and sometimes only to one. Some persons even report seeing strange swirls of the stuff in their dreams. Others claim being able to touch it physically. Later in the program, we will be discussing the "black dust" phenomenon at length with a panel of experts from different fields . . .

As the radio program continues on to other topics in the background, the attention of the NUNS is diverted to a formless blackness moving spontaneously through the room. At times it appears connected or attached to physical objects. At other times it appears disconnected from them. Like a cloud moving across the fabric of reality itself, the blackness gives form to a deeper dimensionality that paradoxically makes our material reality seem more flat. In other words, the geometry of the black dust represents a connection between the fourth dimension of the world on film and the screen on which the movie is being projected. As the black dust creeps through the NUNS' common area with some seeing it and others not, it passes through/across a crucifix hanging on the wall, causing the painted wounds on the statue of Christ to glisten ambivalently. Some of the NUNS get on their knees and start praying. Others leave the room. SISTER CONNELLY remains calm, a subtle smile and joy appearing on her face.

EXT/INT. A CASTLE IN A DESERT LANDSCAPE – SUNRISE

FRANK and REBECCA stand in front of the White Castle, surrounded by a small film CREW. The White Castle is considerably aged and damaged by time and warfare, with some illegible graffiti. REBECCA is directing the scene.

                    REBECCA

Frank, I can't believe it! We are really here! The final
scene. Our work is nearly finished!
        (she kisses him with joy)

                    REBECCA

Are you ready?

                    FRANK

Absolutely. I runneth over.

                    REBECCA

OK, everyone, places!! Listen carefully. All equipment
off for this scene. Frank is shooting this one himself. He
is the camera and I hold the film, so we cannot have any
interference. Trust me. Everything off. Turn yourself
off!

The CREW all stand in a rough circle some distance away.
FRANK turns to REBECCA.

                    FRANK

See you.

                    REBECCA

Until now.

FRANK and REBECCA give each other a kiss of peace, like
the Templars in the previous scene. REBECCA moves her left
hand to her pocket, where she is holding something in a container. FRANK walks forward at a normal pace, pausing very
slightly before entering the castle and then disappearing slowly inside as all watch in silence.

                    REBECCA
        (with her voice breaking a little)

Cut! Ok, everyone, that is it. We are finished.

REBECCA walks to the back of the castle, with the rest of the CREW following, chatting normally. The camera remains behind, so that we see everyone disappear. The voice of the CREW die down to silence and we see the castle standing empty and silent in the desert wind for a long while. The sun starts to set. Eventually, we hear the sound of an approaching black helicopter. The helicopter lands and MARSILIO BARBI gets out. He inspects the grounds, sees the footprints, and enters the building, finding nothing. He walks around the back, where he sees a human-like cross form drawn in charcoal on the stone wall, just like in the opening scene with the THREE FIGURES. He stares at it for a while, then approaches the wall and places his finger within the black center of the design, pressing on the stone very slightly near where the heart would be to see if he might enter. Nothing doing. It is just stone. But then he suddenly pulls back his hand and shakes it as if burned.

                    MARSILIO
        Sacro cuore . . .

Holding his finger, he looks at the image again, then kicks the dust and goes back into the helicopter, which then flies away into the distance. The camera re-enters the stone building and becomes motionless. A formless black dust, seeming at once in the building and in the materiality of the film itself, swirls strangely through the space.

FADE OUT.

THE END

[1] " . . . after black, / The colours of the Rainbow did appear / The Peacock's-Tayl" (*Marrow of Alchemy*, 2.30).

[2] A red Tau Cross (in St. Francis's hand) and pendant:

[3] "The peacock (*pavo*) takes its name from the sound of its voice. Its flesh is so hard that it barely decays and is difficult to cook" (Isidore, *Etymologies*, 12.7.48). "For who but God the Creator of all things has given to the flesh of the peacock its antiseptic property? This property, when I first heard of it, seemed to me incredible; but it happened at Carthage that a bird of this kind was cooked and served up to me, and, taking a suitable slice of flesh from its breast, I ordered it to be kept, and when it had been kept as many days as make any other flesh stinking, it was produced and set before me, and emitted no offensive smell. And after it had been laid by for thirty days and more, it was still in the same state; and a year after, the same still, except that it was a little more shrivelled, and drier" (Augustine, *City of God*, 21.4).

"*Moriendo renascor* ('In dying I am reborn'). Bone, vine, and phoenix represent the palingeneses of the vegetable and animal kingdoms from their mineral foundation. For Schwaller, the human femur—the largest bone in the body—was the repository of the fixed alchemical salt, the immortal mineral remains that neither fire nor putrefaction can destroy, 'the last in corruption and the first in generation' (Steeb). The incorruptible ashes or salts were regarded by Schwaller as the passive register that preserved an entity's acquired consciousness, and the agent of all mutations between kingdoms and species" (Aaron Cheak, "The Call of Fire: The Hermetic Quest of René Schwaller de Lubicz,"

http://www.aaroncheak.com/call-of-fire/). Photograph by A. Cheak, Èze-sure-mer, 2005.

5 "Not sky, it's a pyramid | Black and super weird | Insides of your own eyelid | All we've ever feared" (https://twitter.com/Nicolam777/status/771883362558541824).

[7] Massacio, *Crucifixion of St. Peter*:

[8] "This Soul is above the law, not contrary to the law" (Marguerite Porete, *The Mirror of Simple Souls*).

[9] "God is all. God knows all, and God does all. When the Avatar proclaims he is the Ancient One, it is God who proclaims His manifestation on earth. When man utters for or against the Avatarhood, it is God who speaks through him. It is God alone who declares Himself through the Avatar and mankind. I tell you all, with my Divine Authority, that you and I are not 'WE,' but 'ONE'" (Meher Baba, 12 September 1954).

[10] "About the ninth hour, Jesus cried out in a loud voice, 'Eli, Eli, lema sabachthani?' which means, 'My God, My God, why have you forsaken Me?' When some of those standing there heard this, they said, 'He is calling Elijah'" (Matthew 27:46-7).

[11] "Now Simon Peter stood and warmed himself. Therefore they said to him, 'You are not also one of His disciples, are you?' He denied it and said, 'I am not!' One of the servants of the high priest, a relative of him whose ear Peter cut off, said, 'Did I not see you in the garden with Him?' Peter then denied again; and immediately a rooster crowed" (John 18:25-7).

[12] Cf. "hell and heaven are both states of bondage *subject to the limitations of the opposites* of pleasure and pain. Both are states whose duration is determined by the nature, amount and intensity of the accumulated impressions. *Time in the subtle world is not the same as time in the gross world due to the increased subjectivity of the states of consciousness*; but though time in the subtle world is thus *incommensurable* with time in the gross world, it is strictly determined by the impressions accumulated in the gross world" (Meher Baba, *Discourses*, III.62).

[13]

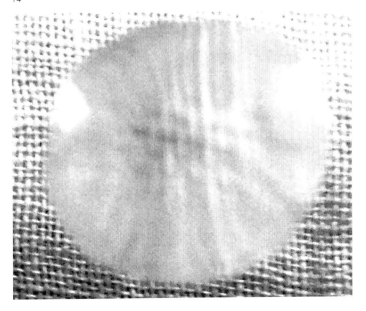

15 "Veramente a così alto sospetto / non ti fermar, se quella nol ti dice / che lume fia tra 'l vero e lo 'ntelletto. / Non so se 'ntendi: io dico di Beatrice; / tu la vedrai di sopra, in su la vetta / di questo monte, ridere e felice" (Dante, *Purgatorio*, 6.43-8) [However, do not desist from from such a deep doubt until she tells you, she who will be a light between the truth and your intellect. I don't know if you understand; I mean Beatrice: you will see her above, on the summit of this mountain, smiling and happy].

16 "The process of perception runs parallel to the process of creation, and the reversing of the process of perception without obliterating consciousness amounts to realising the nothingness of the universe as a separate entity. The Self

sees first through the mind, then through the subtle eye and lastly through the physical eye; and it is *vaster than all that it can perceive*. The big ocean and the vast spaces of the sky are tiny as compared with the Self. In fact, *all that the Self can perceive is finite, but the Self itself is infinite*. When the Self retains full consciousness and yet sees nothing, it has crossed the universe of its own creation and has taken the first step to know itself as everything" (Meher Baba, *Discourses*, II.98).

17

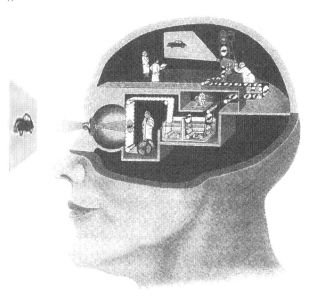

[18] See Nicola Masciandaro, "Decapitating Cinema," in *And They Were Two In One And One In Two*, eds. Nicola Masciandaro & Eugene Thacker (Schism, 2014).

Cf. Salvador Dalí's *Crucifixion (Corpus Hypercubus):*

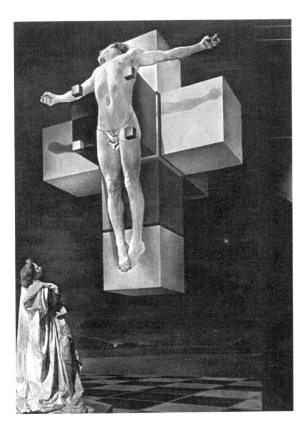

[20] "When we have worn out the interest we once took in death, when we realize we have nothing more to gain from it, we fall back on birth, we turn to a much more inexhaustible abyss" (E. M. Cioran, *The Trouble with Being Born*).

[21] "No one to worry = nothing to worry about" (https://twitter.com/Nicolam777/status/604744574951682049).

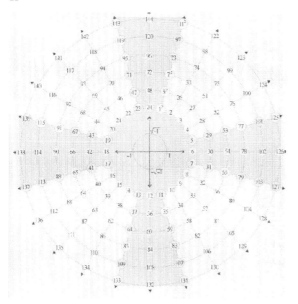

See Peter Plichta, *God's Secret Formula Deciphering the Riddle of the Universe and the Prime Number Code* (Element Books, 1997). "But then we have this emergence into consciousness of the set of the prime numbers buried within the set of positive integers, a hidden archetype within an archetype, a kind of chaos within order, the black dot in the yin half of the yin-yang symbol; the emergence of *that* archetype – the prime numbers, the zeta function, and everything they entail – into mass consciousness, is just starting now, really. … The only thing I can really say with any confidence at all is that I think we're on the verge – and again, the timescale is very indefinite here – but Western civilization is on the verge of collectively realising that the number system is something very different from what it had previously thought it to be. I haven't got a particular theory what it is, I just know it isn't what we think it is" (Matthew Watkins, "Prime Revolution (Interview)," *Collapse* 1 [Urbanomic, 2006]).

23 As Pyrrho is reported by Eusebius to have maintained, "things are equally indifferent and unstable and indeterminate; for this reason, neither our sensations nor our opinions tell the truth or lie. For this reason, then, we should not trust them, but should be without opinions and without inclinations and without wavering, saying about each single thing that it no more is than is not or both is and is not or neither is nor is not" (Eusebius, *Praeparatio evangelica*, XIV.18).

 24

"The ceremony begins with long mystic preliminaries during which the celebrant tramples down all passions and crucifies his selfishness. Then the celebrant blows his bone trumpet, calling the hungry demons to the feast he intends to lay before them. He envisions a female deity, who esoterically personifies his own will, and who springs from the top of his head and stands before him, sword in hand. With one stroke she cuts off the head of the *naljorpa*. Then, while troops of ghouls crowd around for the feast, the goddess severs his limbs, skins him, and rips open his belly. The bowels spill, the blood gushes forth, and the hideous guests bite and chew noisily, while the celebrant excites and urges them on with the liturgic words of unreserved surrender: 'For ages, in the course of renewed births I have borrowed from countless living beings – at the cost of their welfare and life – food, clothing, all kinds of services to sustain my body, to keep it joyful in comfort and to defend it against death. Today, I pay my debt, offering for destruction this body which I have held so dear. I give my flesh to the hungry, my blood to the thirsty, my skin to clothe those who are naked, my bones as fuel to those who suffer from cold. I give my happiness to the unhappy ones. I give my breath to bring back the dying to life. Shame on me if I shrink from giving my *self*! Shame on you, wretched and demoniac beings, if you do not dare to prey upon I . . .'" (Alphonso Lingis, "Dreadful Mystic Banquet," *Janus Head* 3 [2000]).

25

[26] "I heard, then, that at Naucratis, in Egypt, was one of the ancient gods of that country, the one whose sacred bird is called the ibis, and the name of the god himself was Theuth. He it was who invented numbers and arithmetic and geometry and astronomy, also draughts and dice, and, most important of all, letters. Now the king of all Egypt at that time was the god Thamus, who lived in the great city of the upper region, which the Greeks call the Egyptian Thebes, and they call the god himself Ammon. To him came Theuth to show his inventions, saying that they ought to be imparted to the other Egyptians. But Thamus asked what use there was in each, and as Theuth enumerated their uses, expressed praise or blame, according as he approved or disapproved. The story goes that Thamus said many things to Theuth in praise or blame of the various arts, which it would take too long to repeat; but when they came to the letters, 'This invention, O king,' said Theuth, 'will make the Egyptians wiser and will improve their memories; for it is an elixir of memory and wisdom that I have discovered.' But Thamus replied, 'Most ingenious Theuth, one man has the ability to beget arts, but the ability to judge of their usefulness or harmfulness to their users belongs to another; and now you, who are the father of letters, have been led by your affection to ascribe to them a power the opposite of that which they really possess. For this invention will produce forgetfulness in the minds of those who learn to use it, because they will not practice their memory. Their trust in writing, produced by external characters which are no part of themselves, will discourage the use of their own memory within them. You have invented an elixir not of memory, but of reminding; and you offer your pupils the appearance of wisdom, not true wisdom, for they will read many things without instruction and will therefore seem to know many things, when they are for

the most part ignorant and hard to get along with, since they are not wise, but only appear wise'" (Plato, *Phaedrus*).

[27] "This has been the theme of my life ever since: love – horror, horror – love: one worse than the other" (Ladislav Klima, *Glorious Nemesis*).

[28]

[29] See Jame McClenon and Emily D. Edwards, "The Incubus in Film, Experience, and Folklore," *Southern Folklore* 52.1

(1996): 3-18. "The creature is said to produce evil dreams (nightmares) by sitting on the chest of the sleeper. These dreams might be carnal in nature, or they might simply involve a sense of suffocation or oppression . . . It is the night-*rider*, the creature that rides the man or woman to love or death . . . The nightmare is the incubus or succubus" (Stan Gooch, *The Origins of Psychic Phenomena: Poltergeists, Incubi, Succubi, and the Unconscious Mind*).

30

31

32

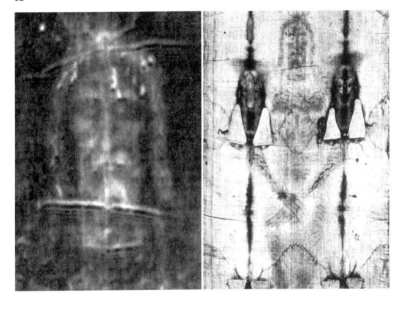

33

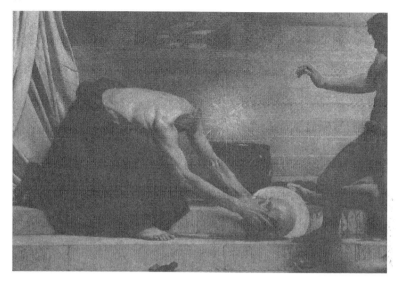

34

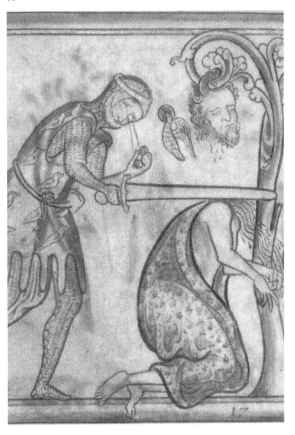

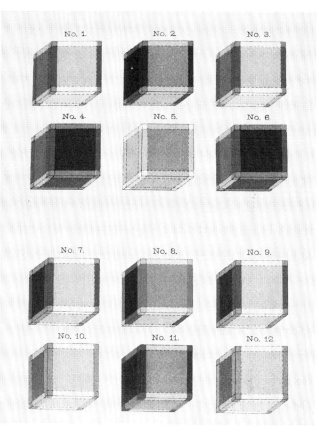

EXAMEN CONSCIENTIAE.

1. Gratias age 2. Pete lumen. 3. Examina 4. Dole 5. Propone.

CONSCIENTIÆ
Generale.

PRo comperto ponitur, triplex incidere homini cogitationum genus : unum ex proprio surgens mente ipsius hominis : Reliqua verò duo extrinsecus advenientia , ex boni scilicet , vel mali spiritûs suggestione.

De Cogitatione.

DUobus modis elicitur meritum ex malâ cogitatione, in materiâ peccati mortalis, de quâ hîc sermo est. *Primò,* quando suggeritur de patrando mortali crimine cogitatio, sed eà confestim repugnando vincitur. ..... *Secundò,* quando pravæ istiusmodi suggestioni semel, ac iterum repulsæ , & subinde nihilominus revertenti, continuâ resistitur homo , donec penitùs expugnetur : quod quidem victoriæ genus , meritò alterum antecedit,

Peccat autem leviter aliquis, seu venialiter , quando in subortâ peccati mortalis cogitatione, aliquantulùm moratur, quasi auscultando : vel quando aliqua obiter tenuis delectatione afficitur , vel in eà retundendâ se se exhibet negligentem. Mortale verò peccatum , per cogitationem duobus modis admittitur. *Primò,* quando cogitationi peccati præbetur quacumque ratione assensus. *Secundò* , quando peccatum illud opere completur : idque gravius est priore , ex triplici causâ : videlicet , ob maiorem temporis decursum : ob actum intentiorem : & ob plurima denique offendicula, sive detrimenta.

De loquela.

D

ARKANA

D. E. HARDING

ON HAVING
NO HEAD

ZEN AND THE RE-DISCOVERY
OF THE OBVIOUS

FOREWORD BY HUSTON SMITH

O. D. 50.

[42] See Michelle Karnes, *Imagination, Meditation, and Cognition in the Middle Ages* (University of Chicago Press, 2011).

[43] See Nicola Mascianaro and Anna Kłosowksa, "Between Angela and Actaeon: Dislocation," *L'Esprit Créateur* 50 (2010): 91-105.

Ghous, عوث *s. m.* A title of Mahometan saints, whose ardour of devotion, according to vulgar tradition, is such, that in the act of worship their head and limbs fall asunder.

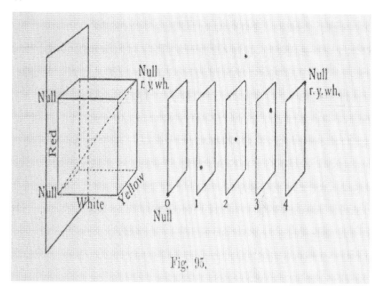

Fig. 95.

[45] "What then will we say? Does it not seem that this degree of love (*amoris*) turns a man's mind to madness, as it were, when it will not allow him to hold a limit or measure to his jealous love (*emulatione*)? Does it not appear to be the height of madness to spurn true life, to reject the highest wisdom, and to resist omnipotence?" (Richard of St. Victor, *On the Four Degrees of Violent Love*).

[49] "This steryng was mikel to forsakyn, and nevertheless mornyng and sorow I made therefor without reason and discretion. But Jesus, that in this vision enformid me of all that me nedyth, answerid by this word, and seyd: *Synne is behovabil, but al shal be wel, and al shal be wel, and al manner of thyng shal be wele.* In this nakid word *synne,* our Lord browte to my mynd generally al that is not good, and the shamfull dispite and the utter nowtyng that He bare for us in this life, and His dyeng, and al the peynys and passions of al His creatures, gostly and bodily – for we be all in party nowtid, and we shall be nowtid followyng our Master Jesus till we be full purgyd, that is to sey, till we be fully nowtid of our dedly flesh and of al our inward affections which arn not very good – and the beholdyng of this with al peynys that ever wern or ever shal be; and with al these I understond the passion of Criste for most peyne and overpassyng. And al this was shewid in a touch, and redily passid over into comforte. For our good Lord wold not that the soule were afferd of this uggly syte" (Julian of Norwich, *Shewings*).

51 "Death by individuation | Perfect upside down | Headless translation | Empyrean crown" (https://twitter.com/Nicolam777/status/7485067749367848 97).

52 "When you know that every problem is only a false problem, you are dangerously close to salvation" (E. M. Cioran, *The New Gods*).

53

54

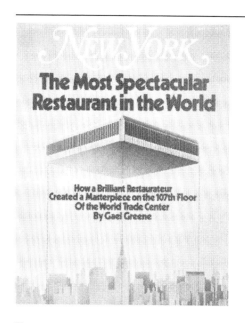

The Most Spectacular Restaurant in the World

How a Brilliant Restaurateur
Created a Masterpiece on the 107th Floor
Of the World Trade Center
By Gael Greene

[55] Cf. "From the initial meetings with Sai Baba and Upasni Maharaj in 1915, Merwan started a grim habit which was to last the entire seven years of his coming down to normal consciousness. Every day Merwan would regularly strike his forehead on the stone floor of his room for hours. Some days in the afternoon, between one and five o'clock, he would go to the Golibar area of Poona or to the isolated Pataleshwar Cave Temple. At the Tower of Silence, sitting under a tree, he would continue this gruesome ritual – knocking his forehead on a rock or against a stone wall. He was not merely tapping his head on the stone surface, but pounding and pounding his brow upon it with full force – always inflicting a bloody wound. After knocking his head hour after hour against stone, Merwan would collapse. He would then wipe the blood off his face and clean himself, and tie a large kerchief or hand-towel around his forehead

to serve as a bandage and a makeshift turban, thus concealing the wound from his family when he returned home. The local neighbors, and his relatives in particular, thought that, by tying a kerchief around his head, Merwan was complying with some new fashion trend. Little did they know the real reason for wearing the kerchief. Only Merwan's closest friends knew how he spent his mornings and afternoons, but they did not reveal this to Merwan's family, though they themselves did not understand his strange behavior. While in Lahore with the Alfred Theatrical Company, Merwan had also pursued this painful self-inflicted practice. He would manage the company and its performances until late in the night. During the day, when the rest of the group was sleeping, he would rise early and quietly slip away to a deserted place, where he would bang his forehead against a flagstone for hours. To come down from the highest spiritual state of God-consciousness – 'I Am God' – to the normal human consciousness – 'I am a man' – entails unimaginable suffering. This striking of his forehead was somehow a comfort to Merwan during the extreme anguish of his descent from the God state to normal or worldly consciousness. Merwan himself later described these days of seeming agony: "This constant hammering of my head was the only thing that gave me some relief during my real suffering of coming down – which I have repeatedly said is indescribable" (*Lord Meher*, 177).

57 *Monkeyshines* (1889-90):

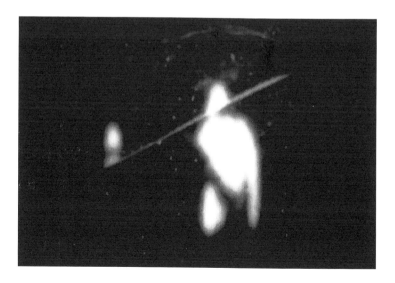

[58] See Nancy Butcher, *The Strange Case of the Walking Corpse* (Penguin, 2004) and Alina Popa, "Dead Thinking," *Bezna* 5 (2014).

[59] "In hell, everything is personalized" (https://twitter.com/Nicolam777/status/260880077477269504).

60

[63] Literally "dancing Judas," referring to the spasms of a hanged man. A favorite exclamation of Italian horror comic hero Dylan Dog.

[64] Cf. Umberto, "Forsaken Dawn," *From the Grave* (2010).

SC⌇SM

Made in the USA
San Bernardino, CA
31 March 2018